THIS BOOK BELONGS TO

°°°°°°°°°°°°°°°°°°°°°°°°°°°°°°°°°

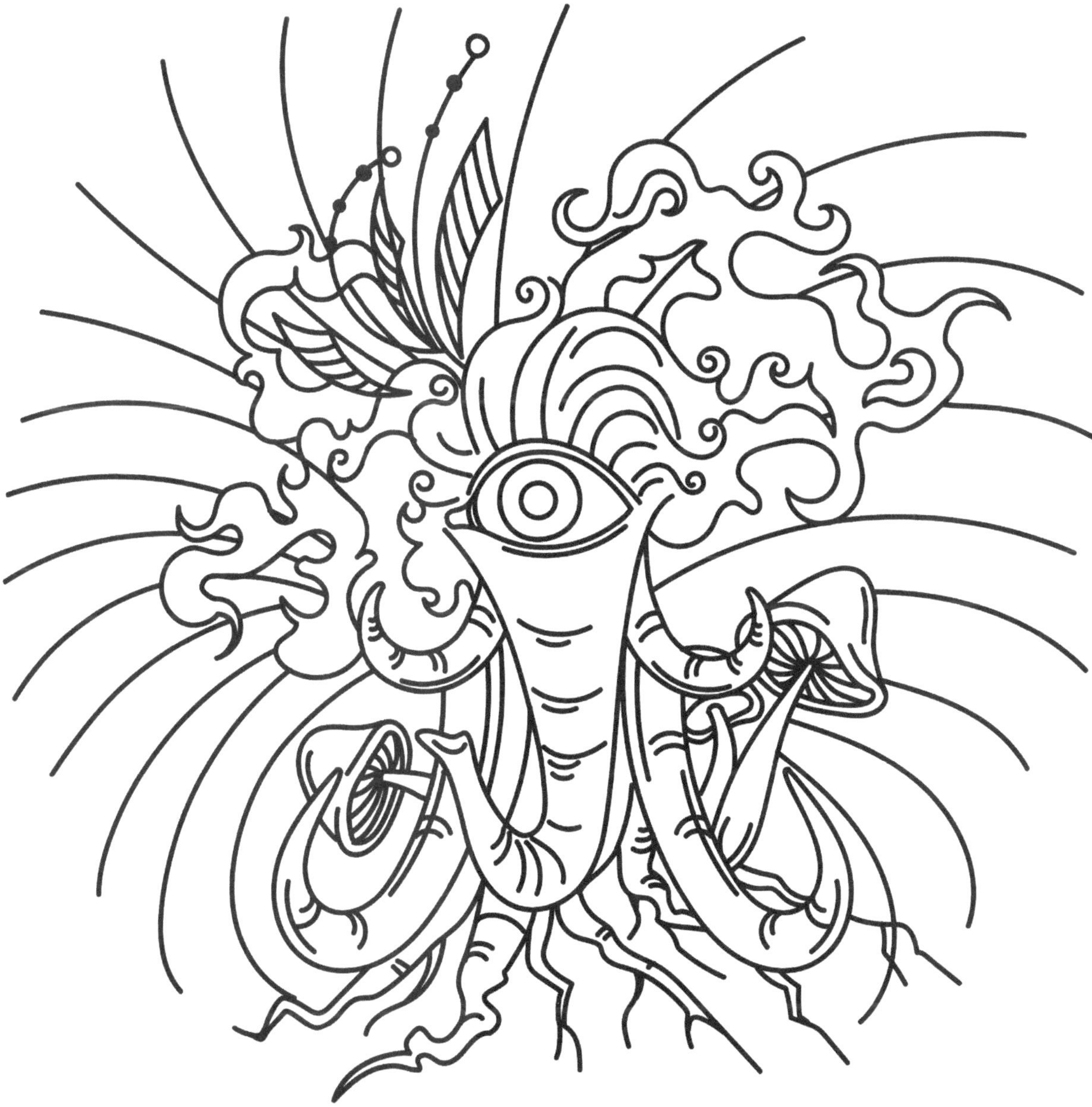

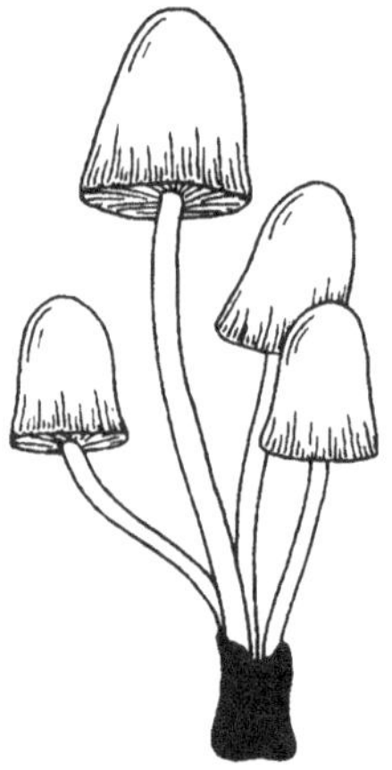

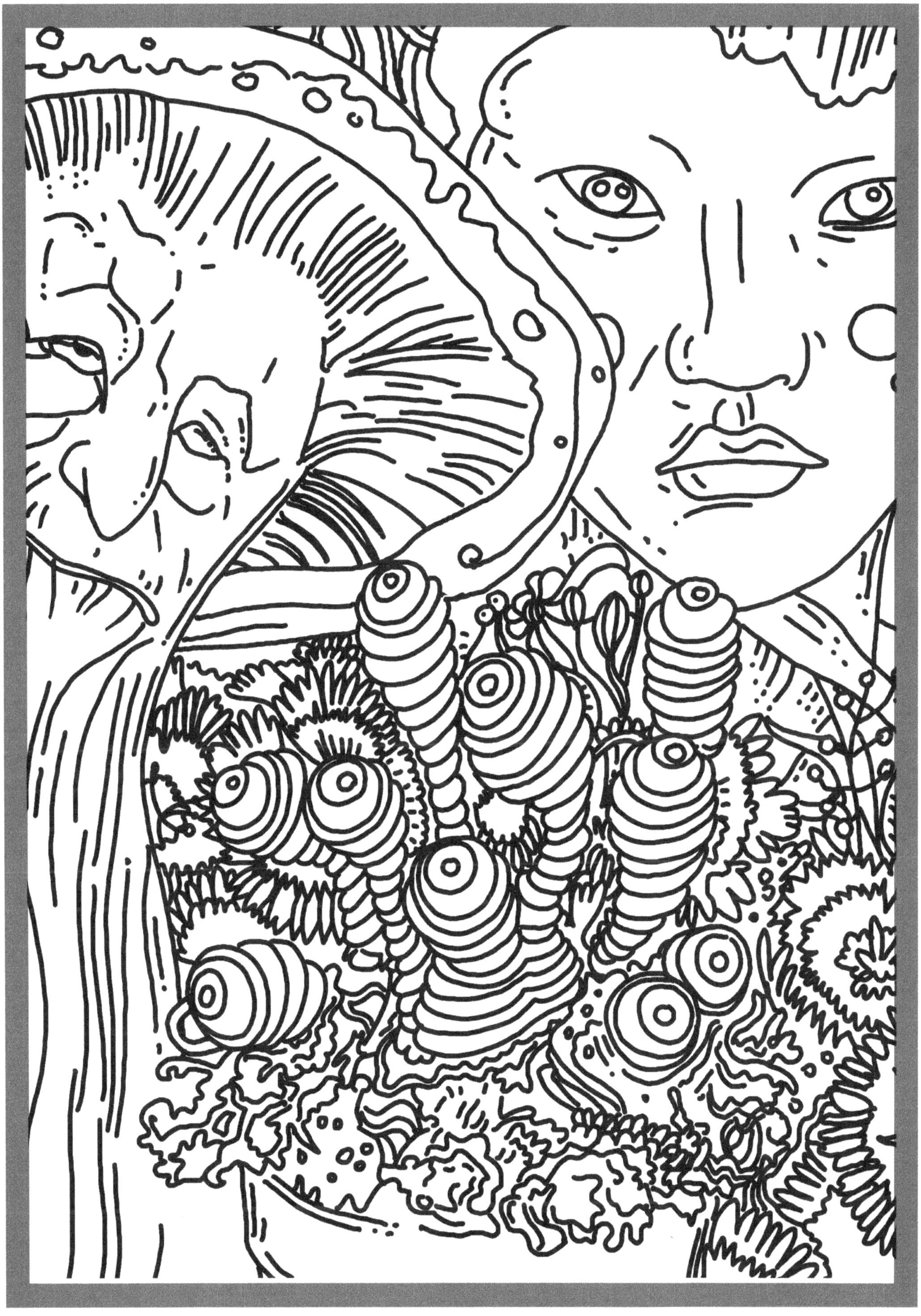

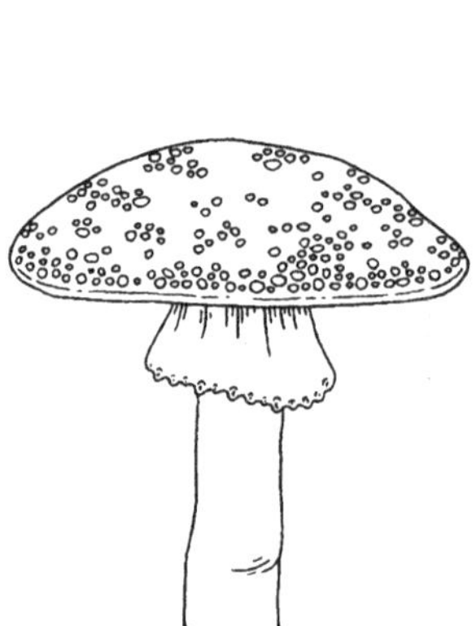

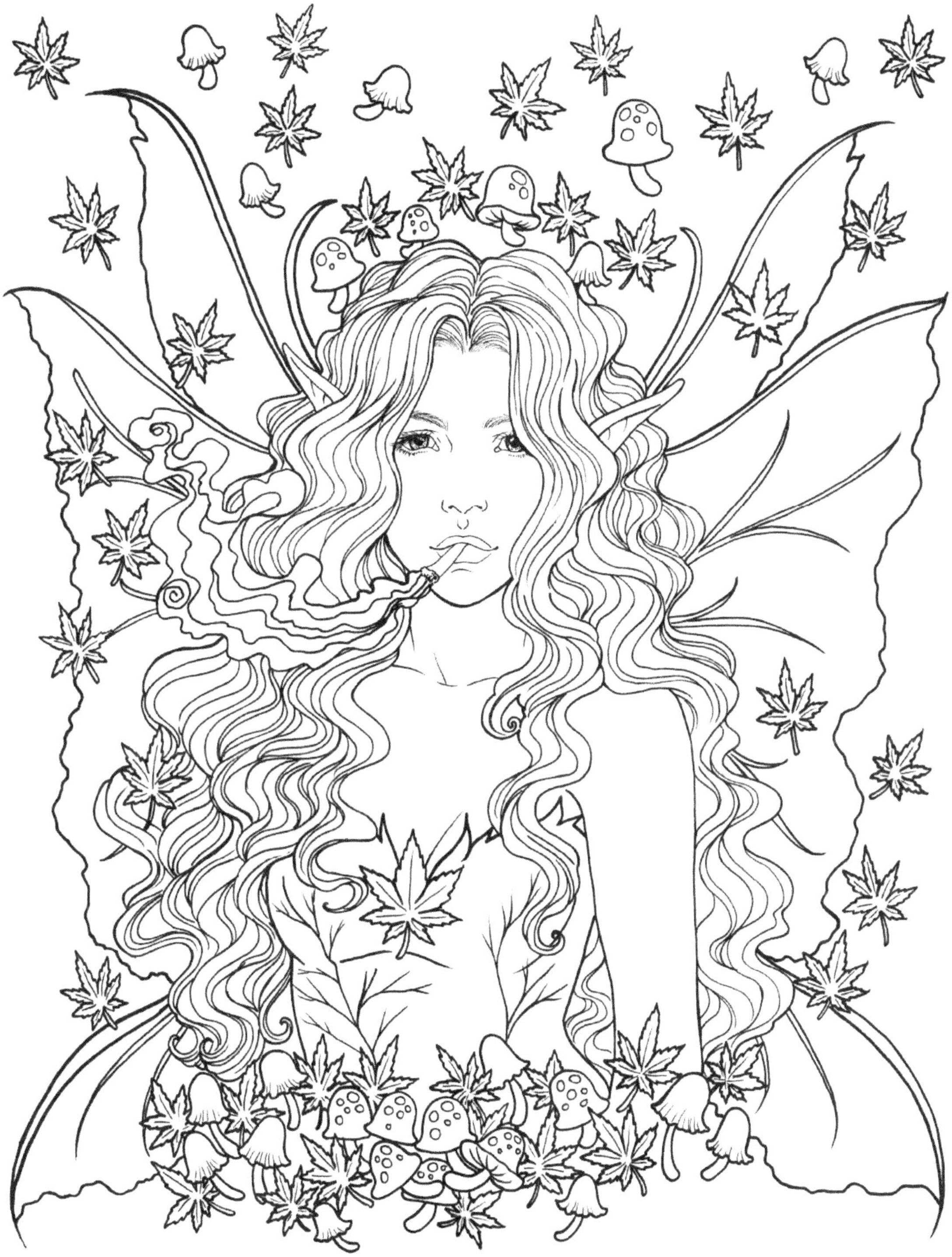

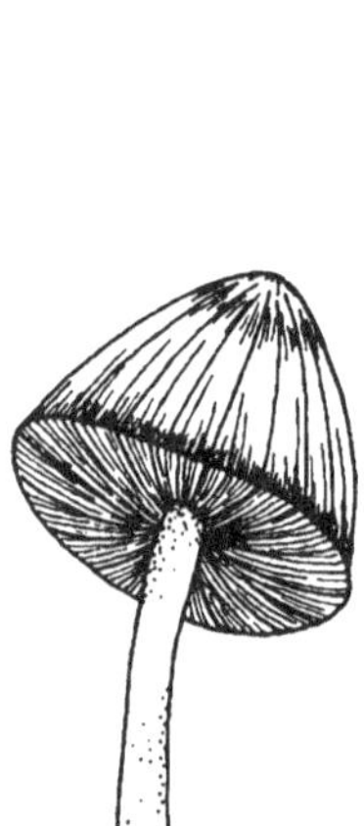

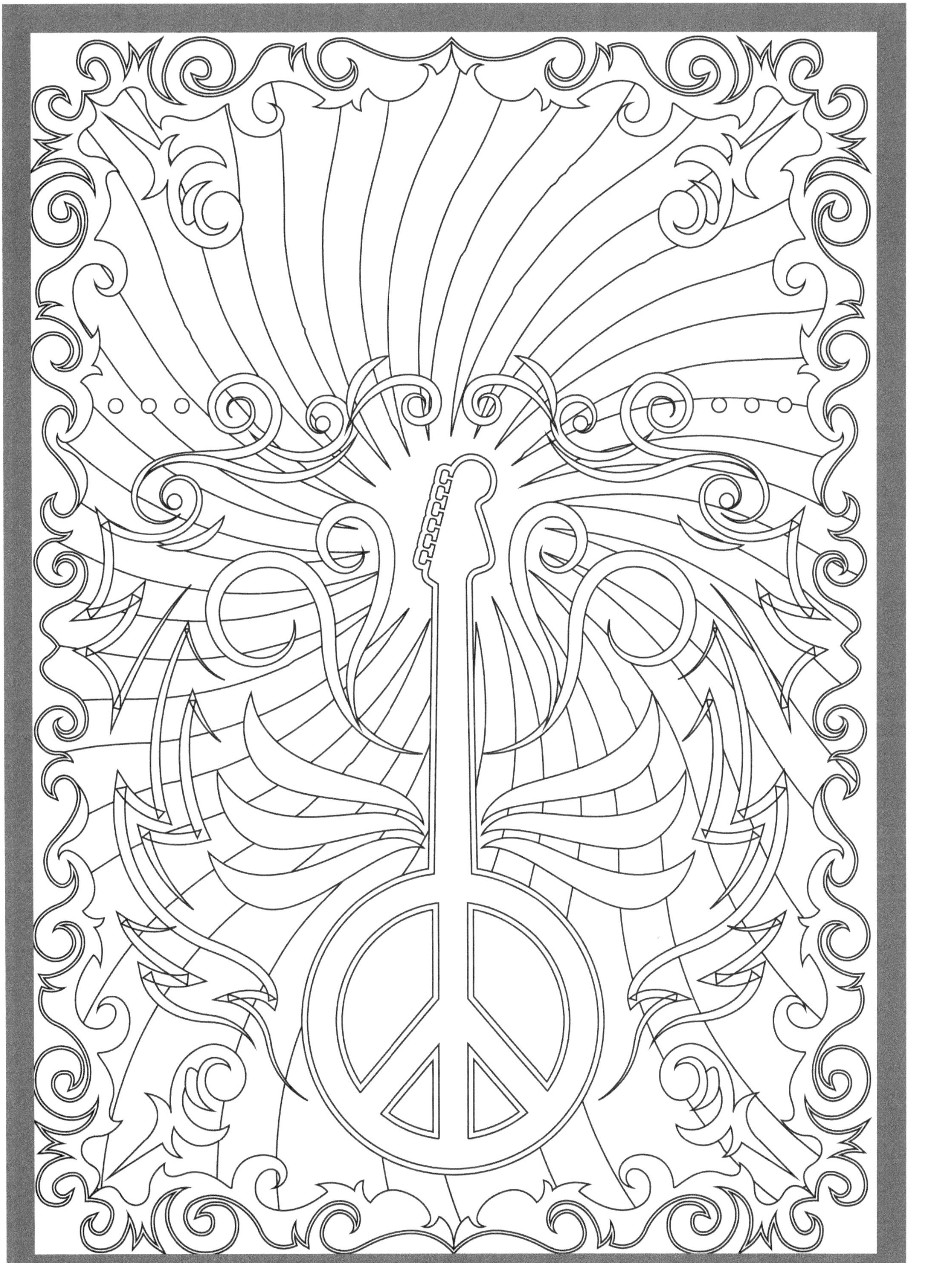

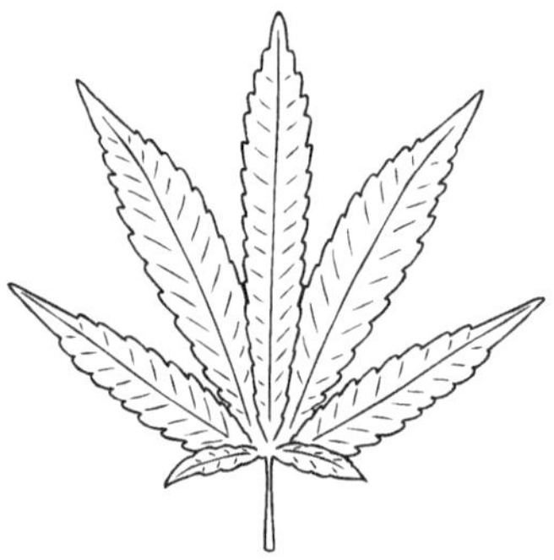

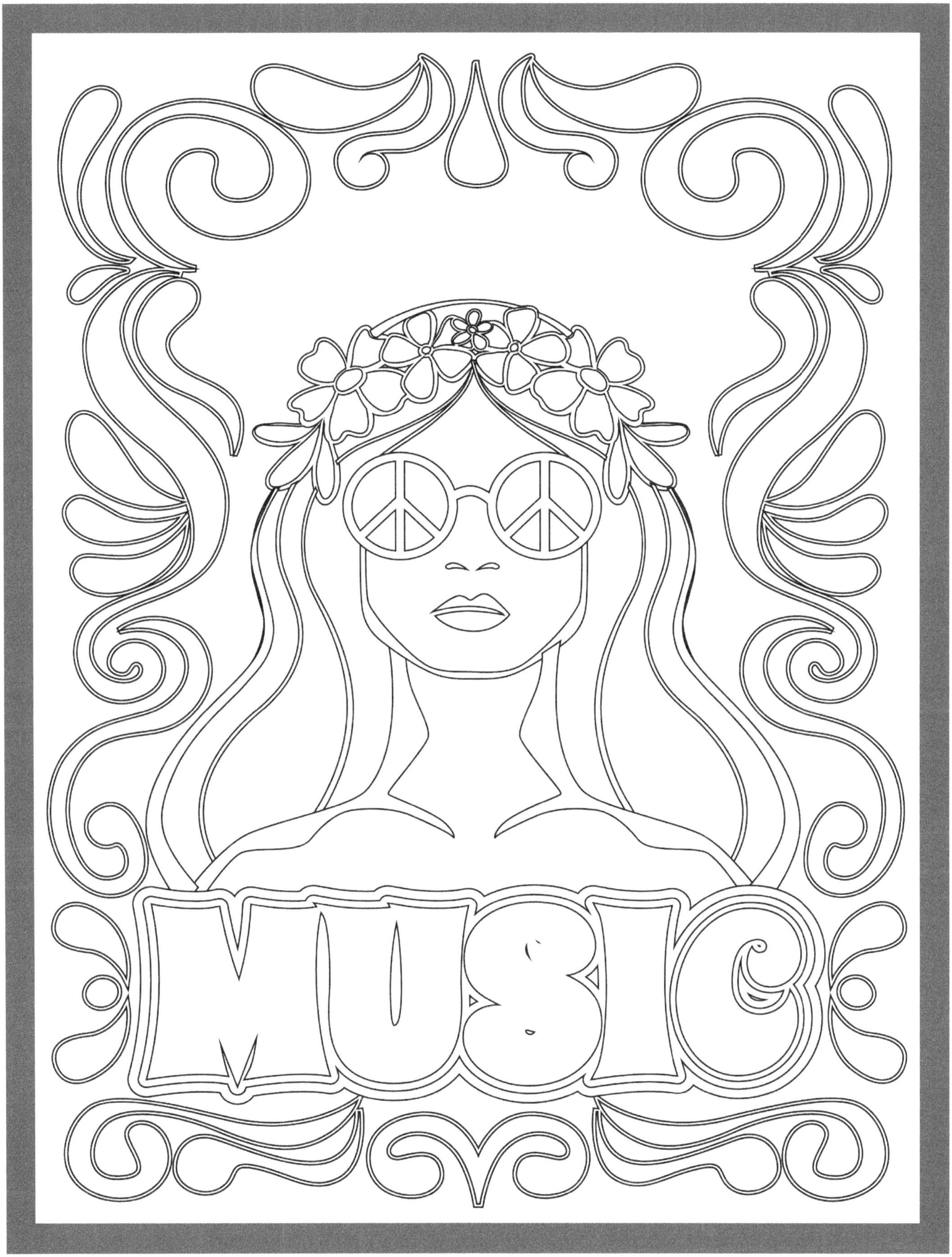
MUSIC

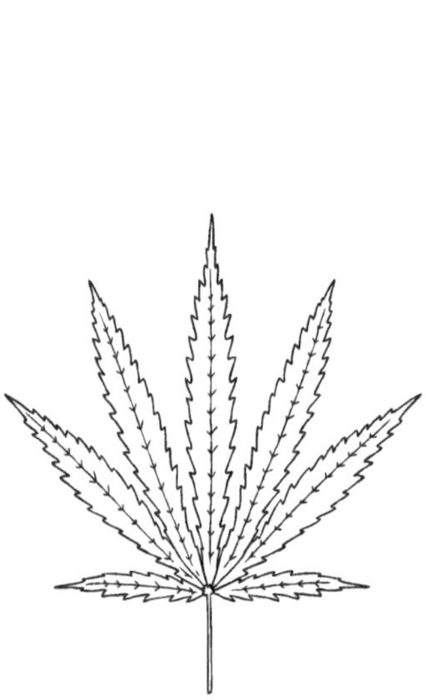

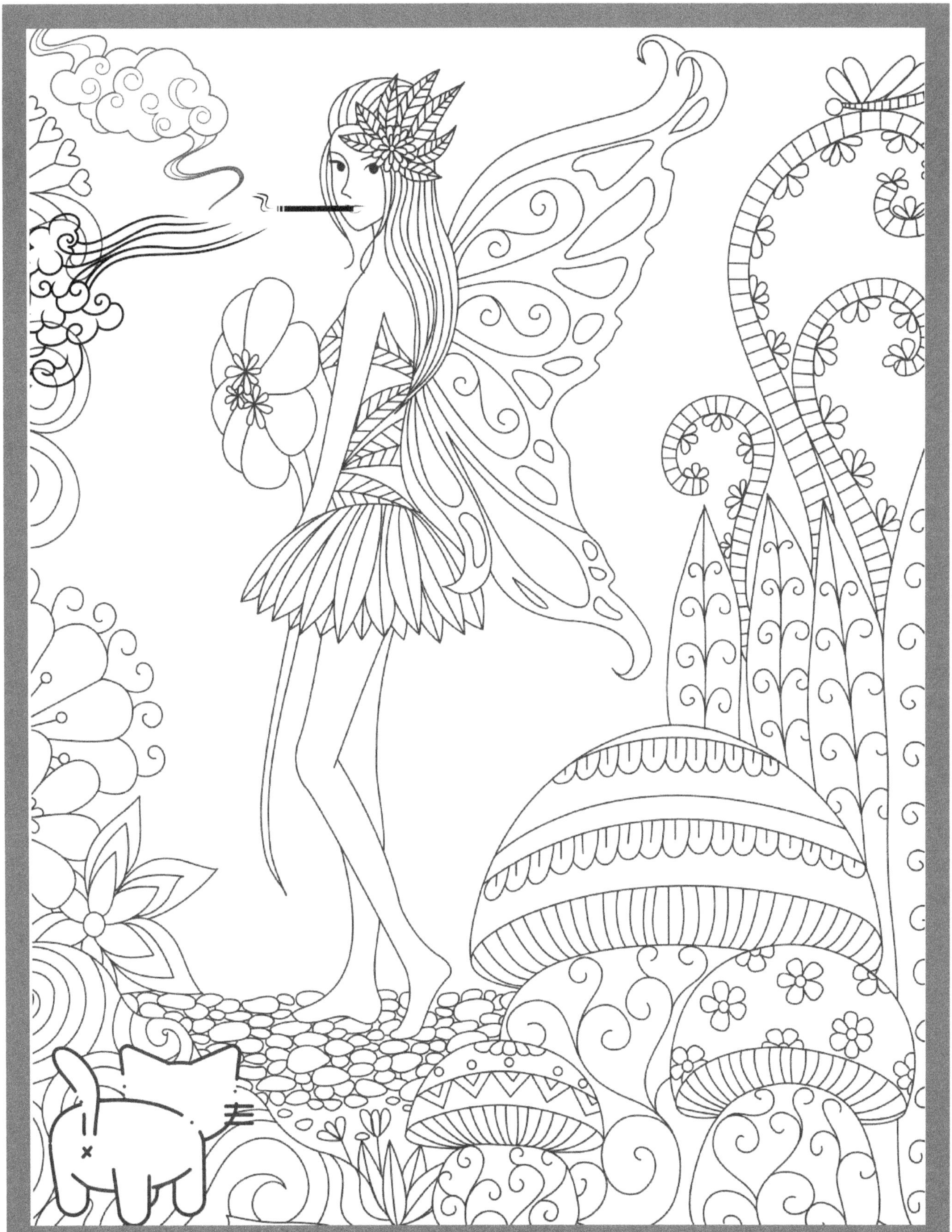

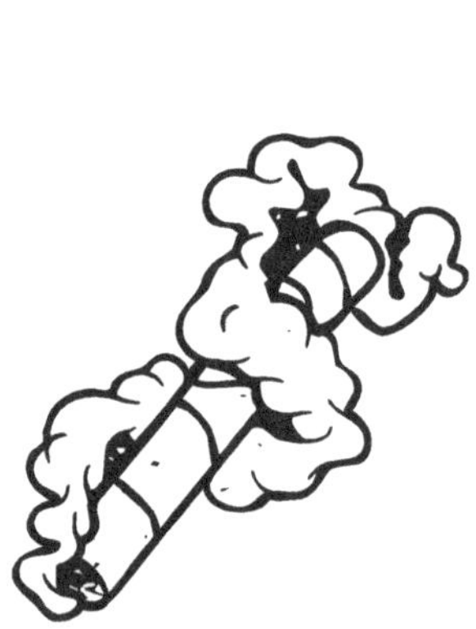

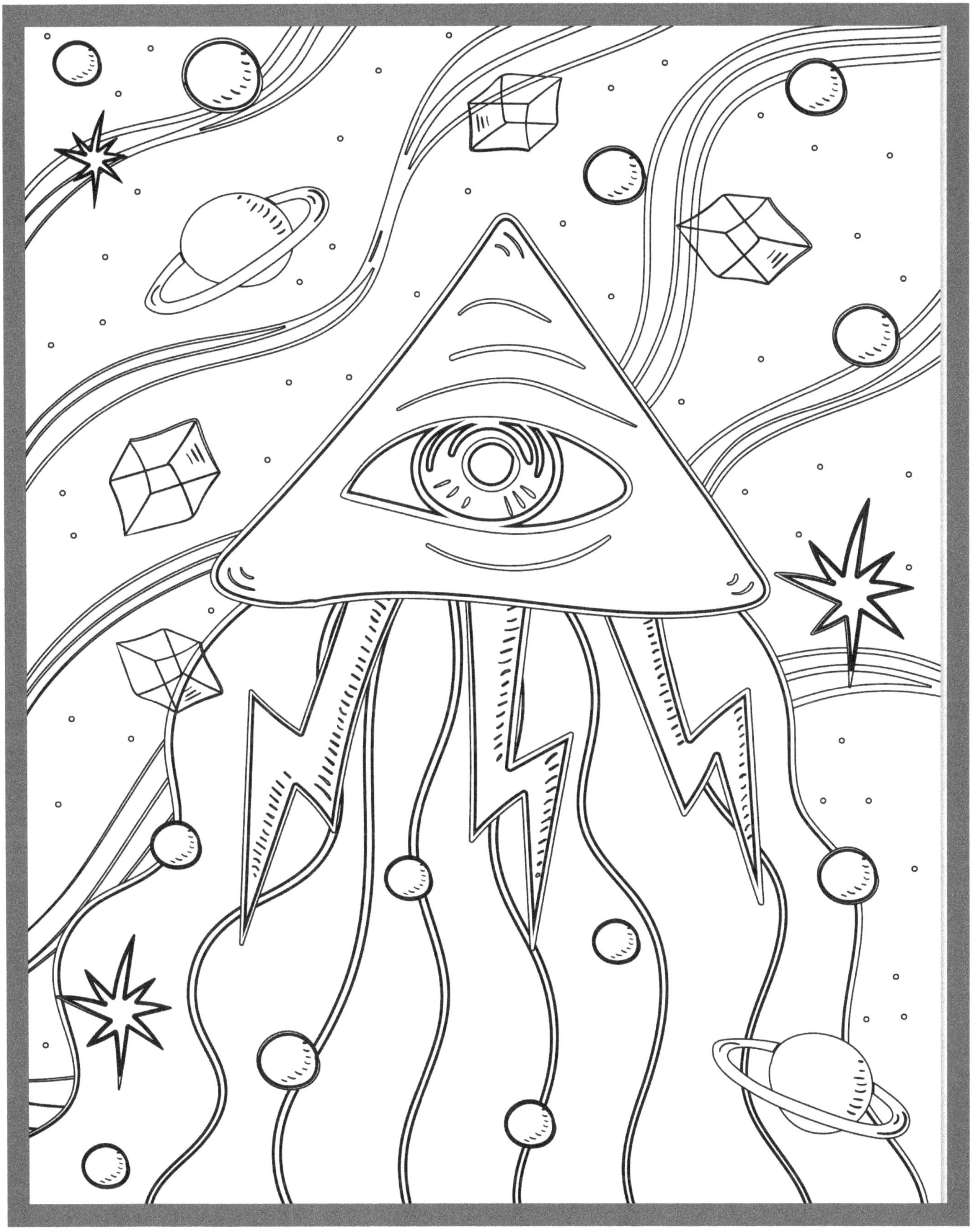

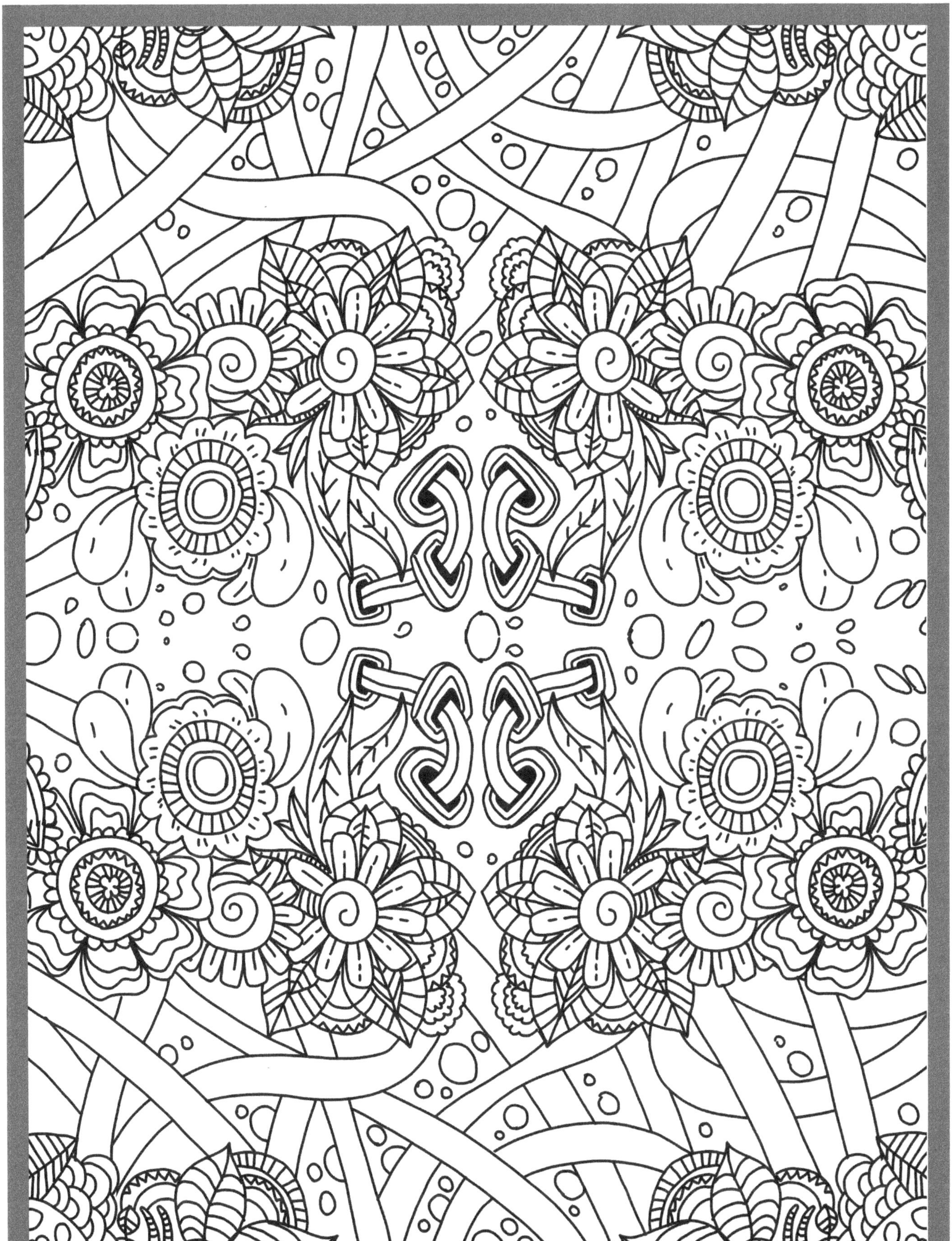

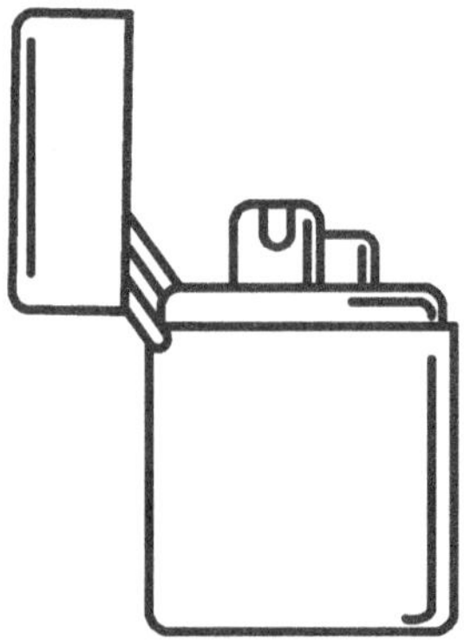

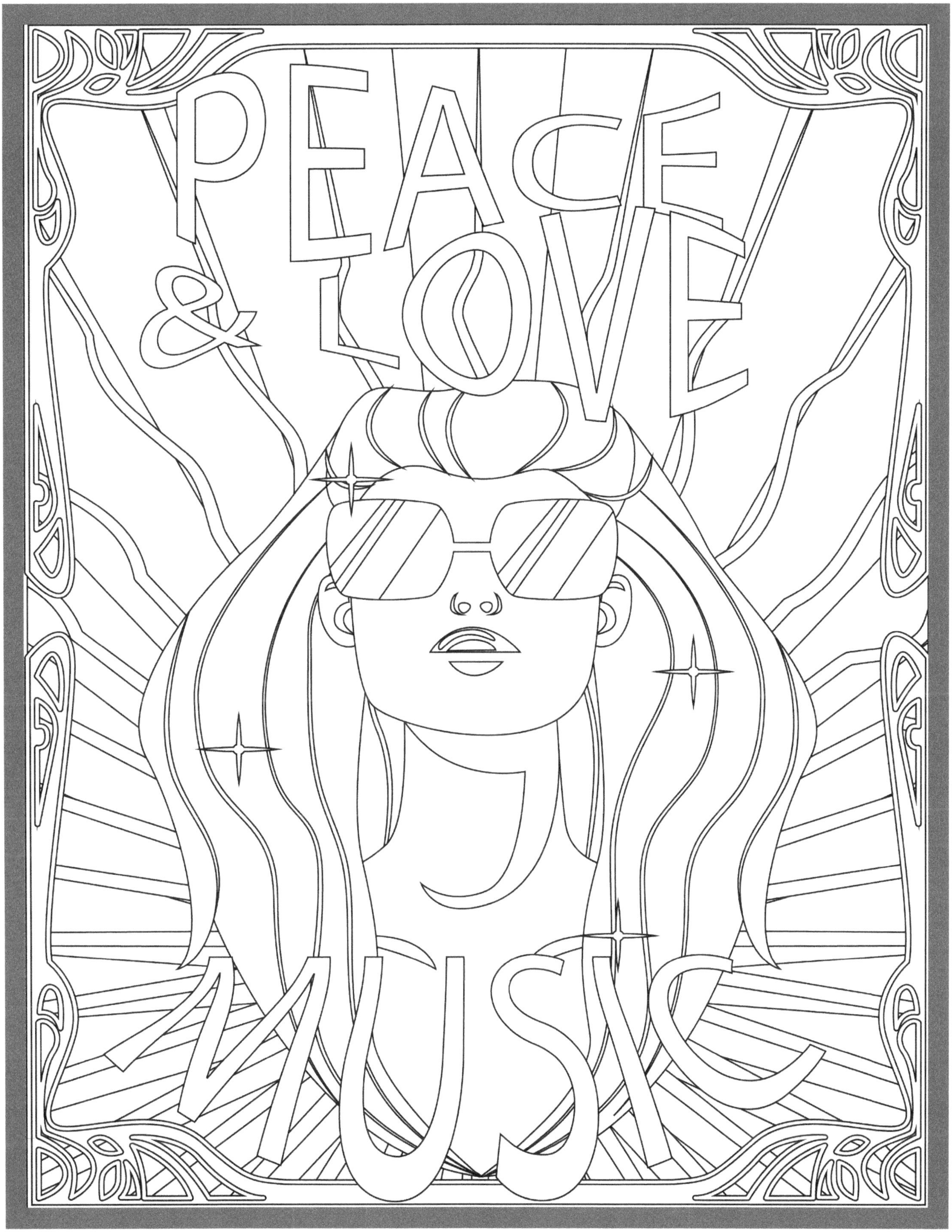
PEACE
& LOVE
MUSIC

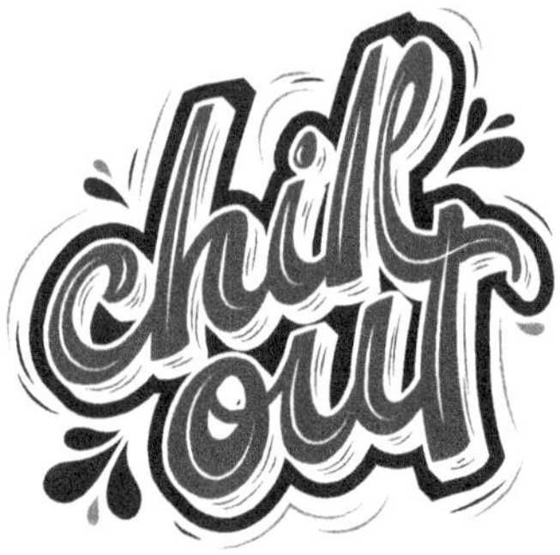
chill out

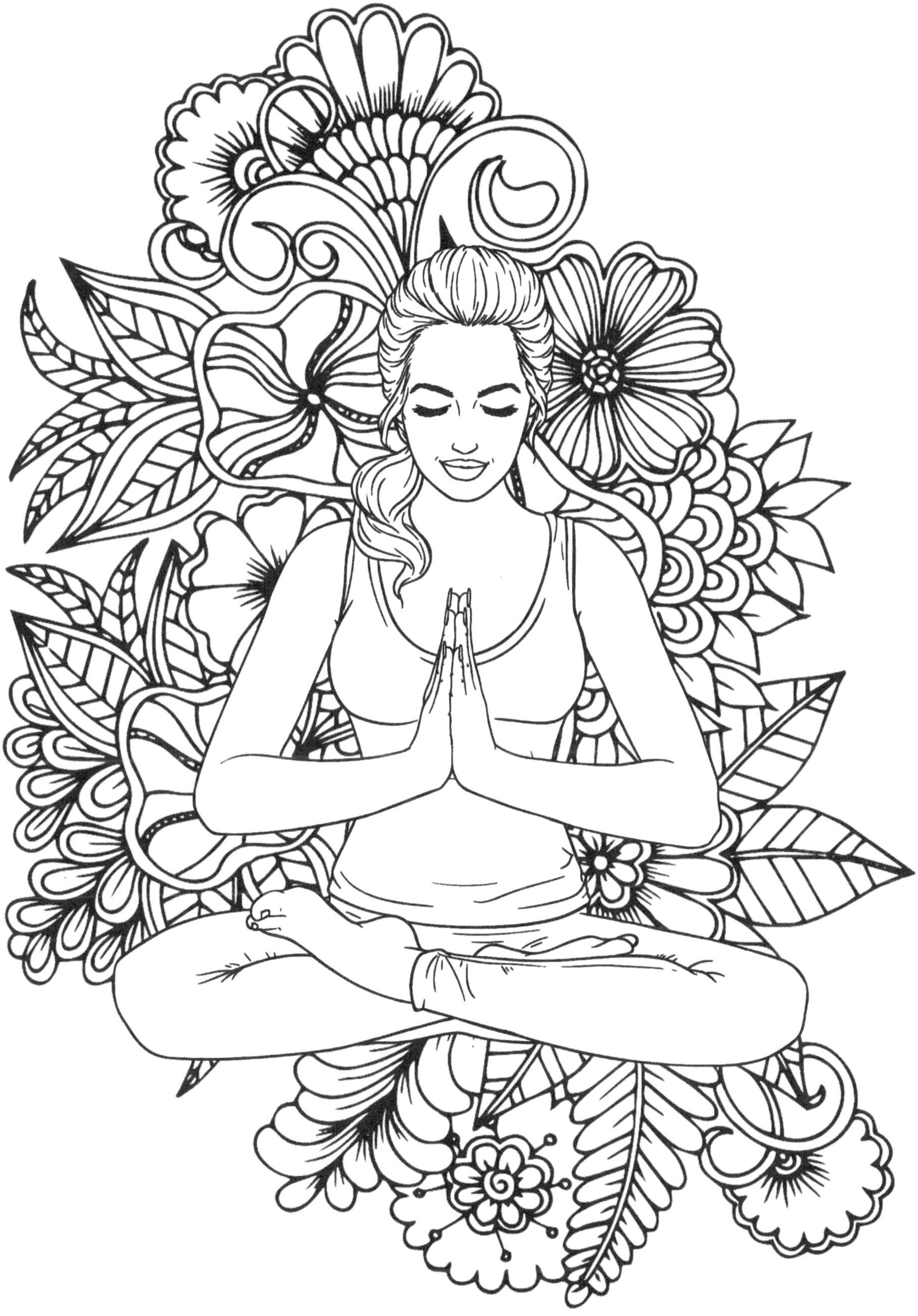

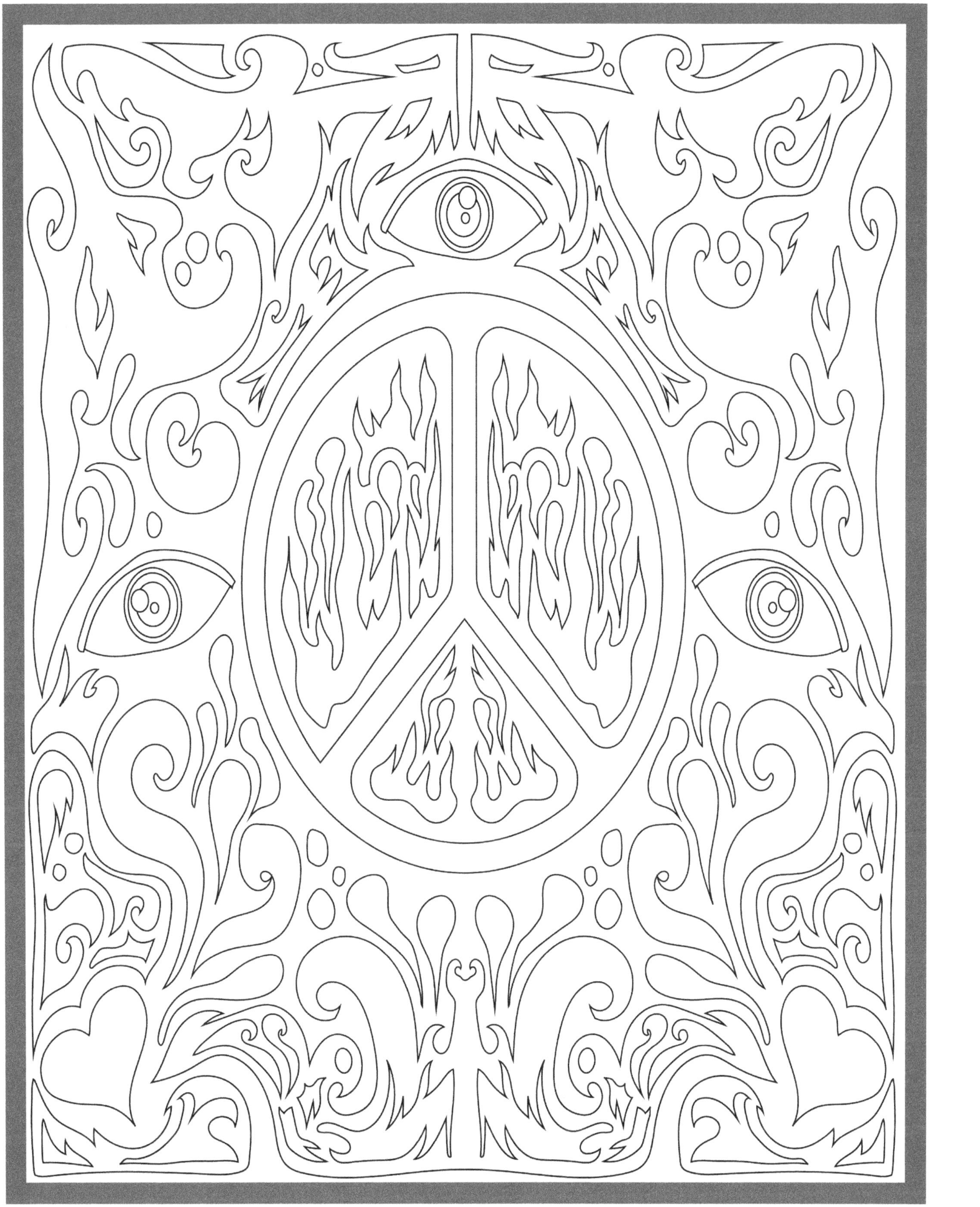

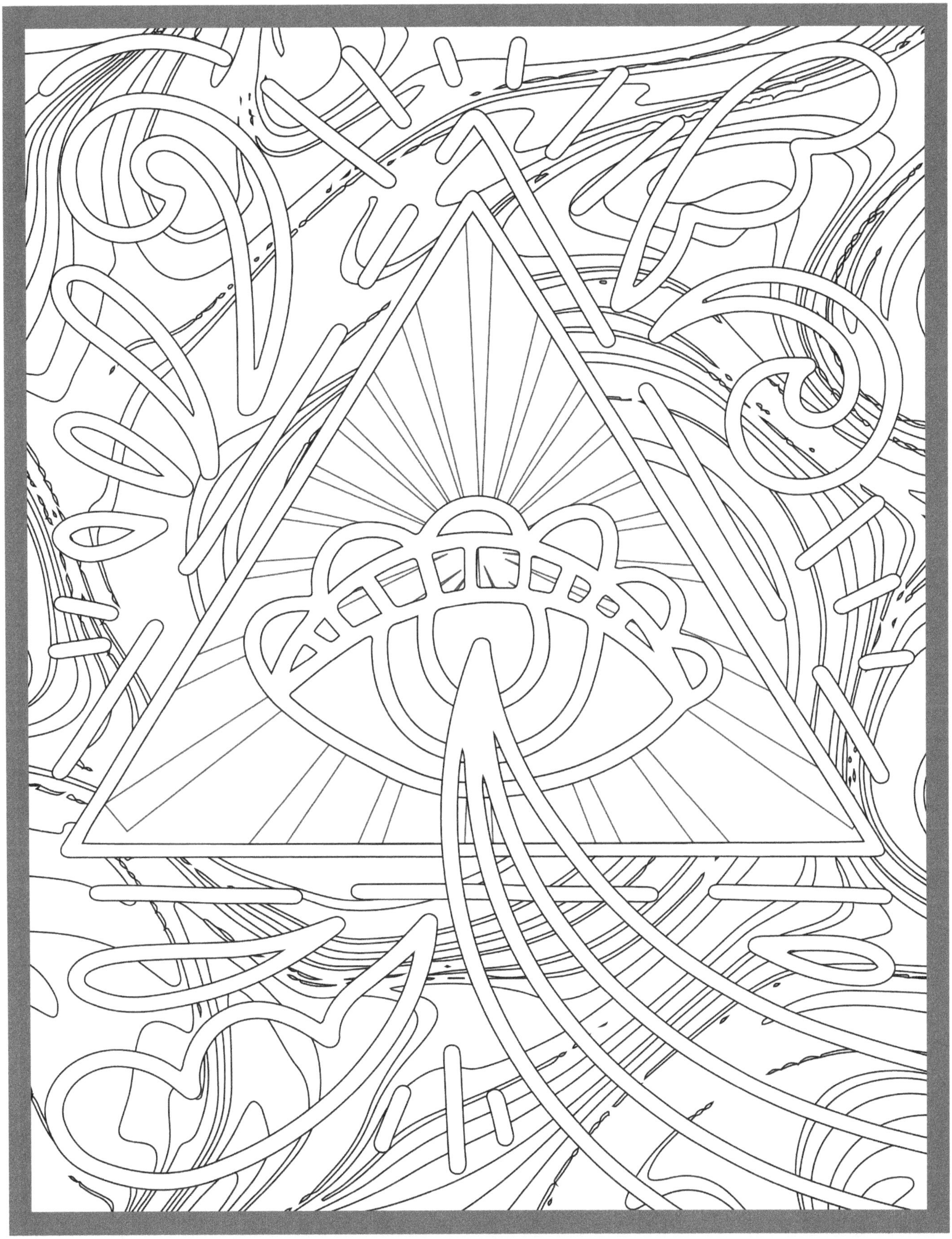

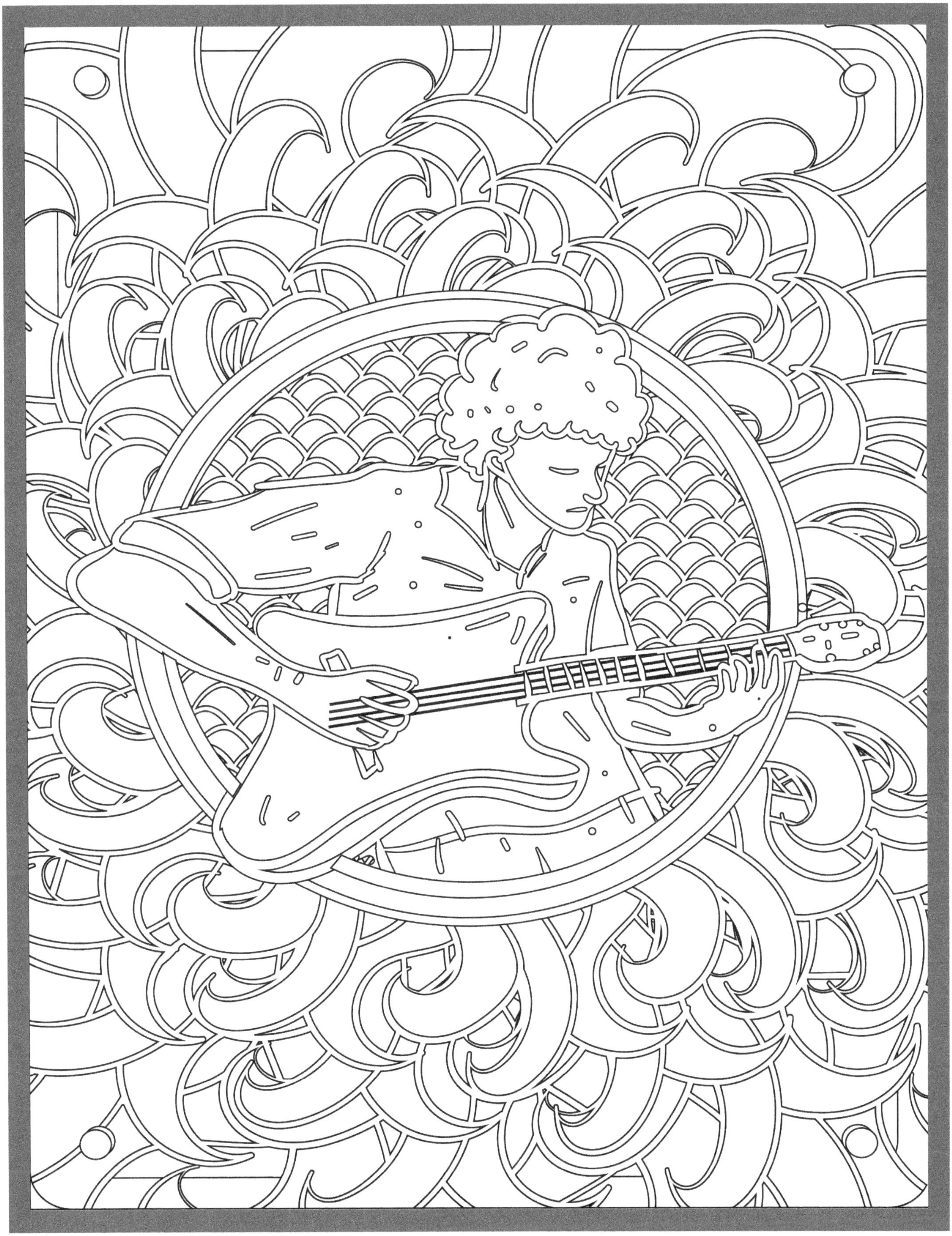

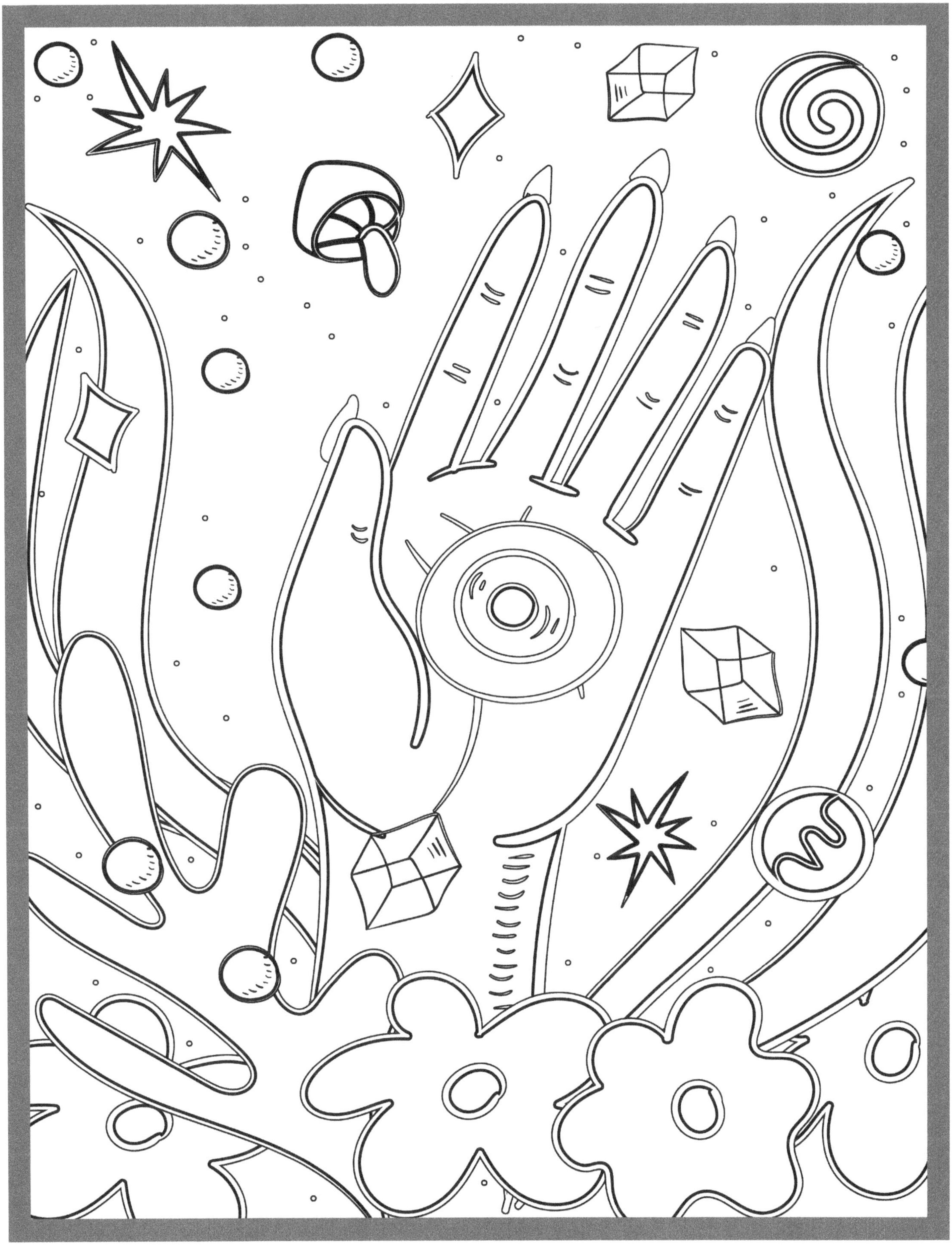

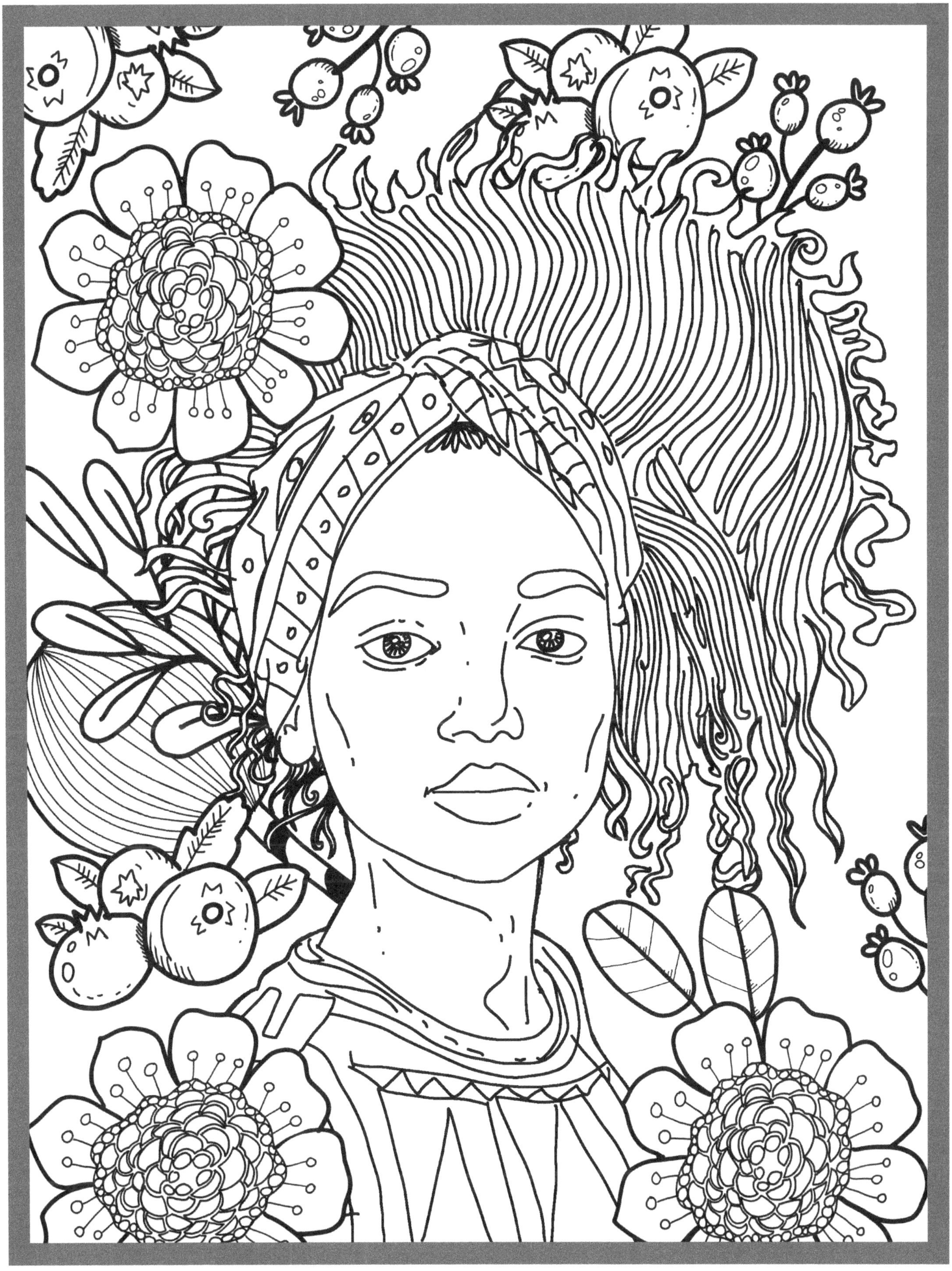

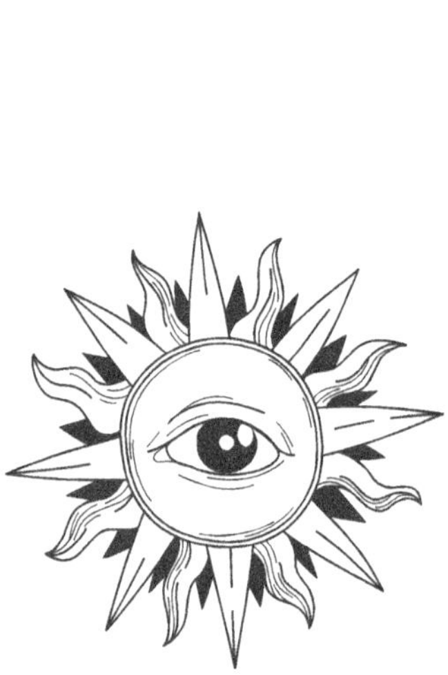

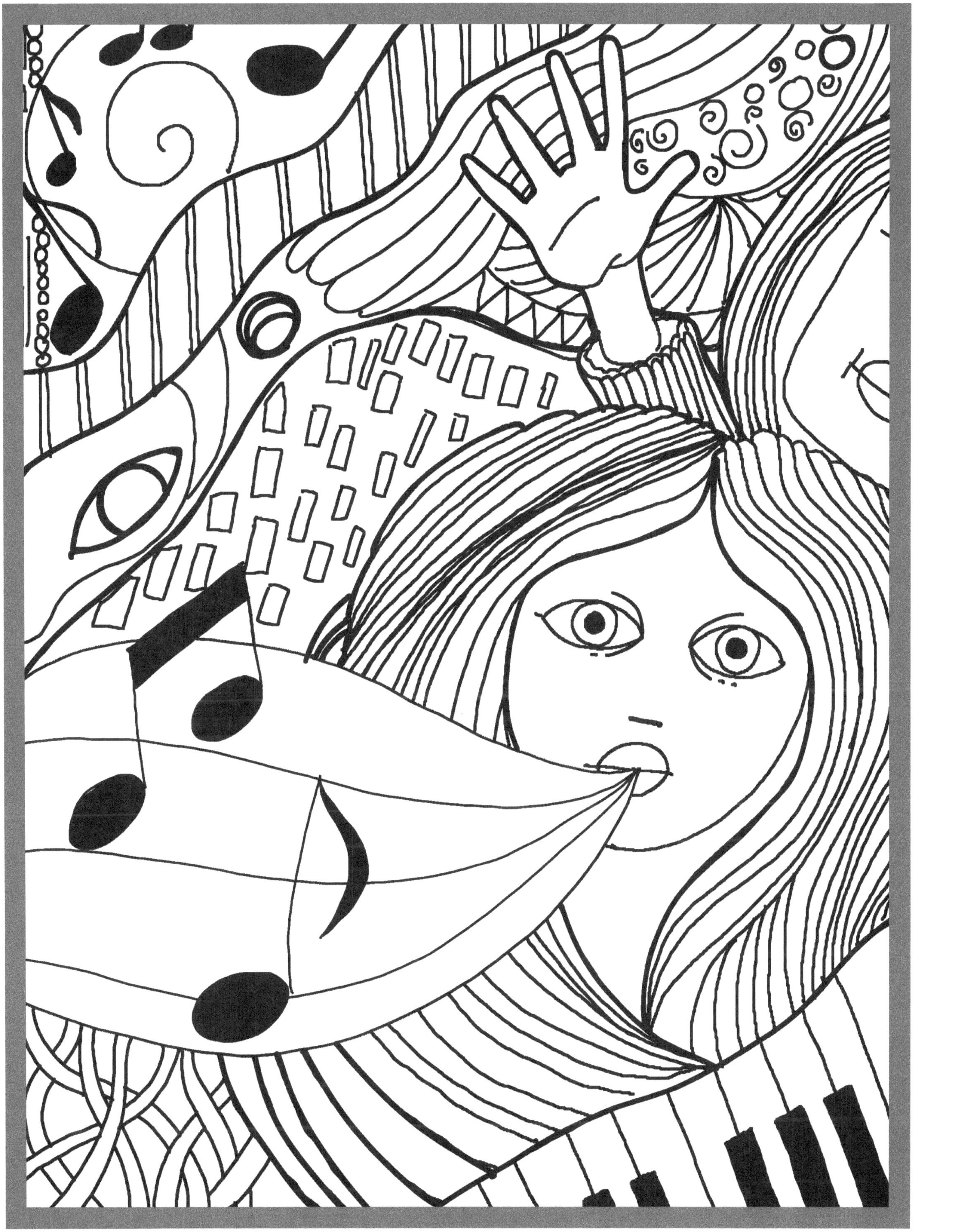

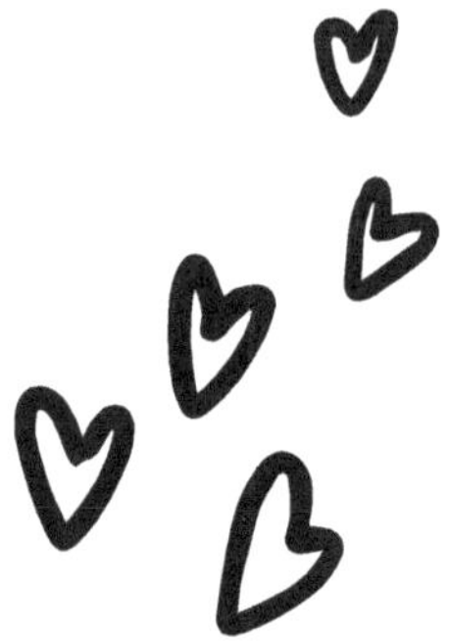

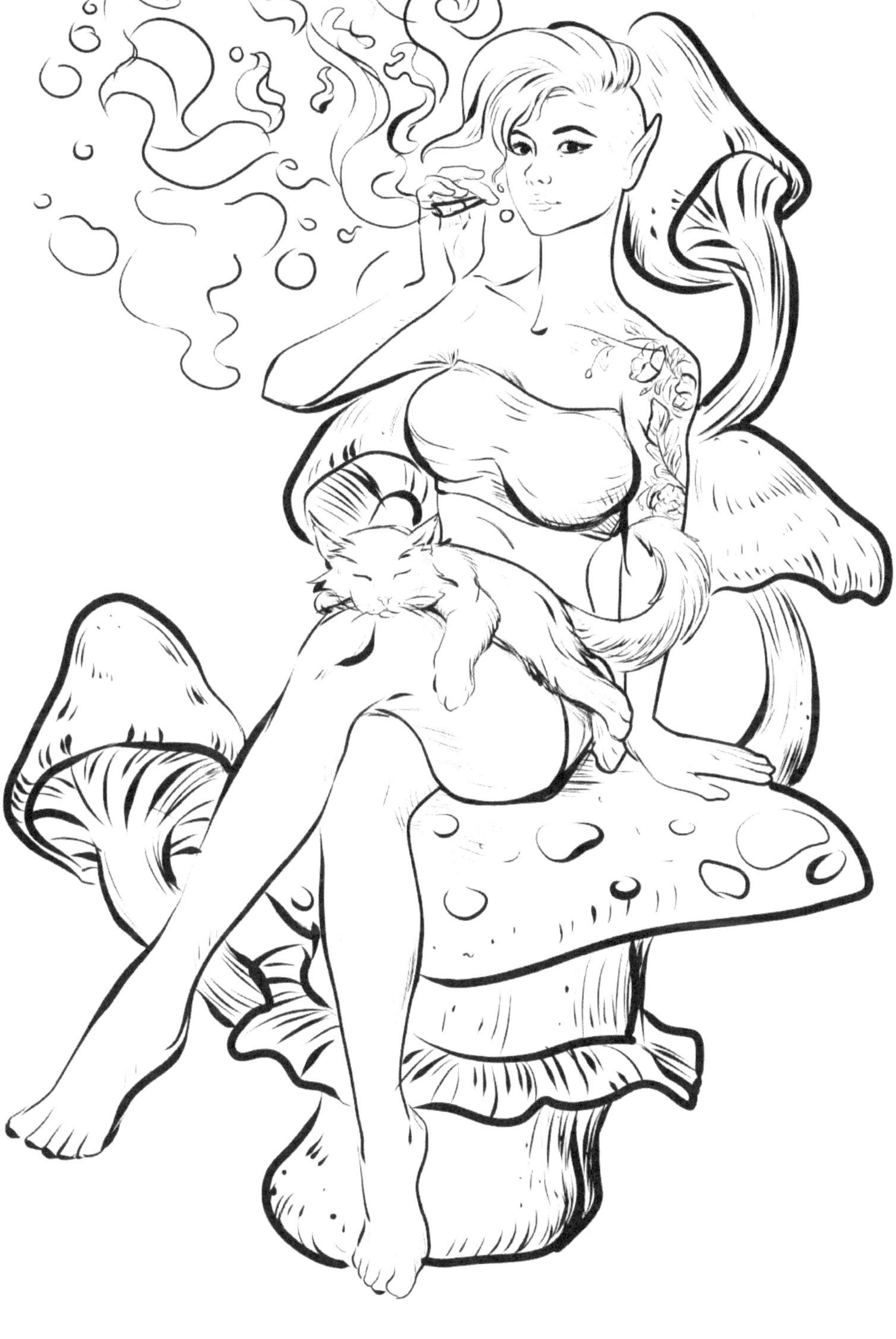

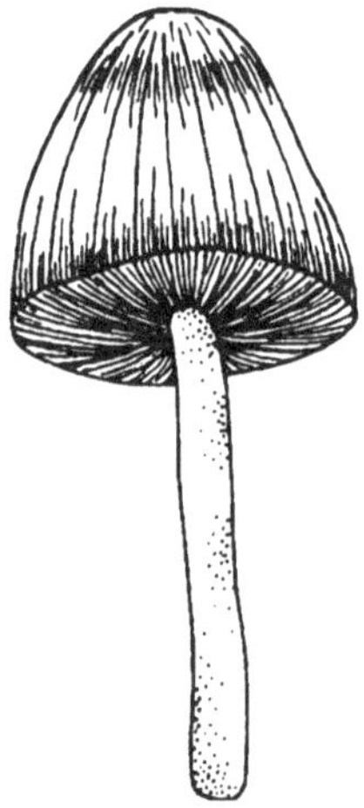

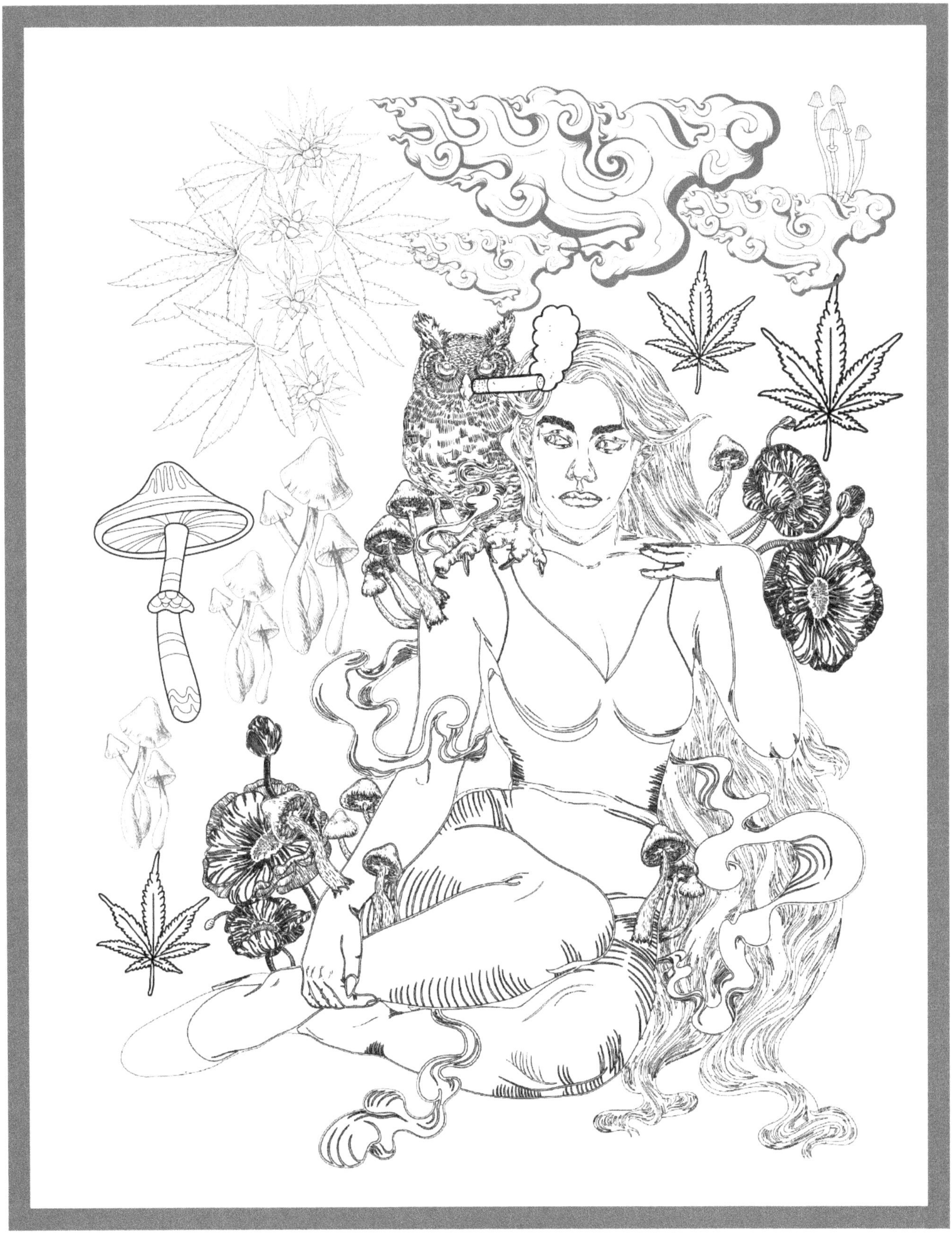

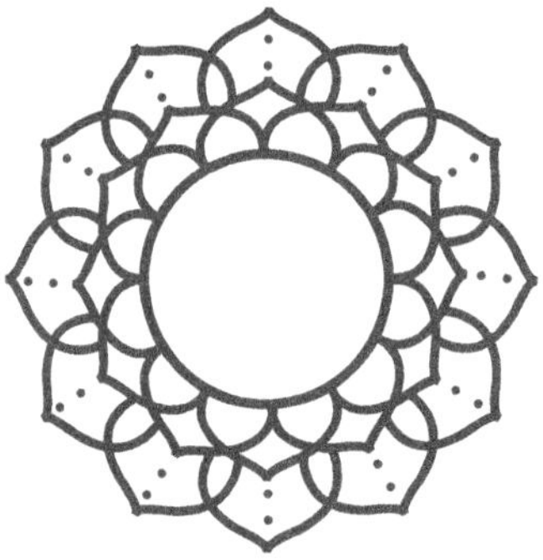

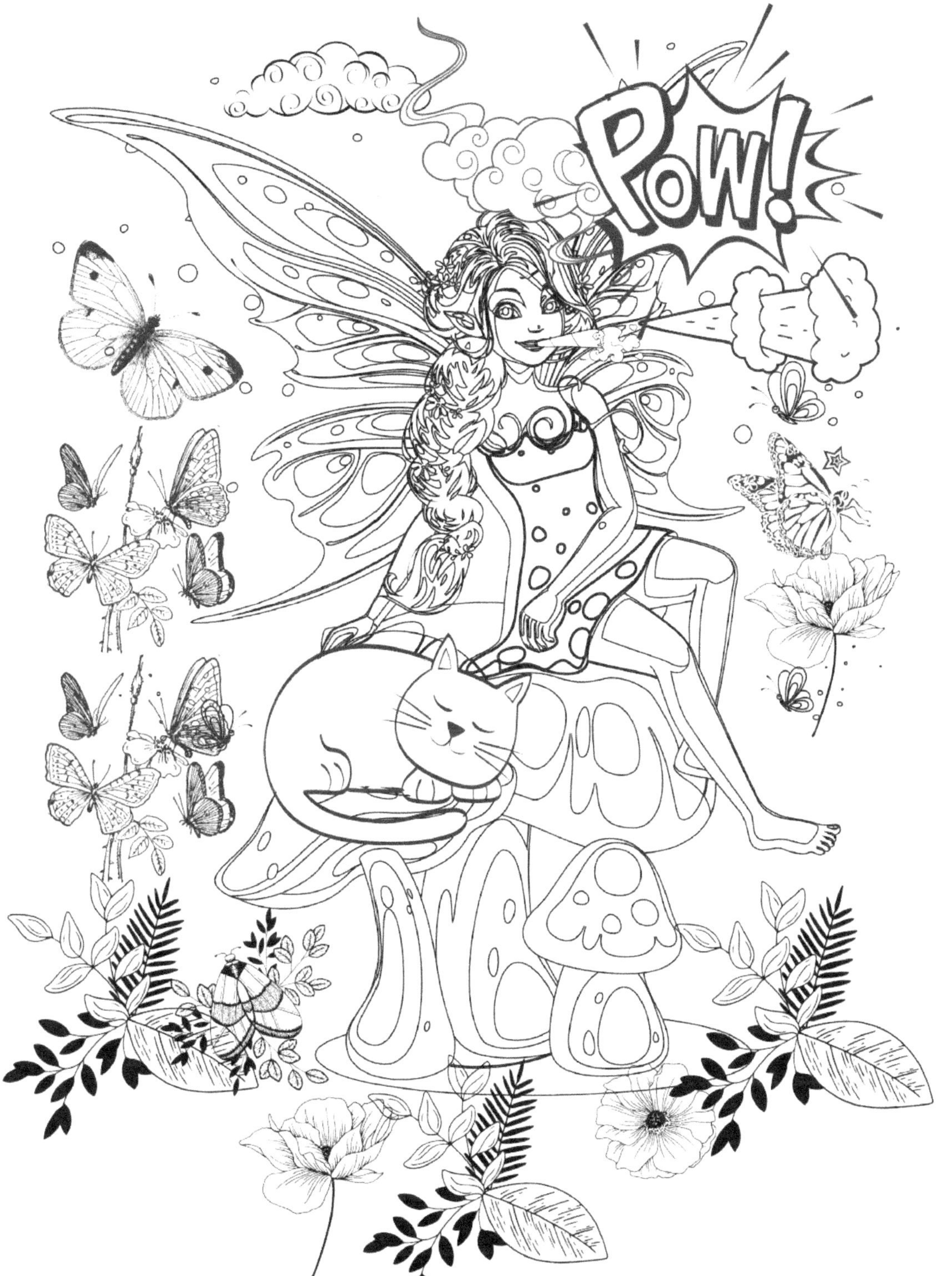
POW!

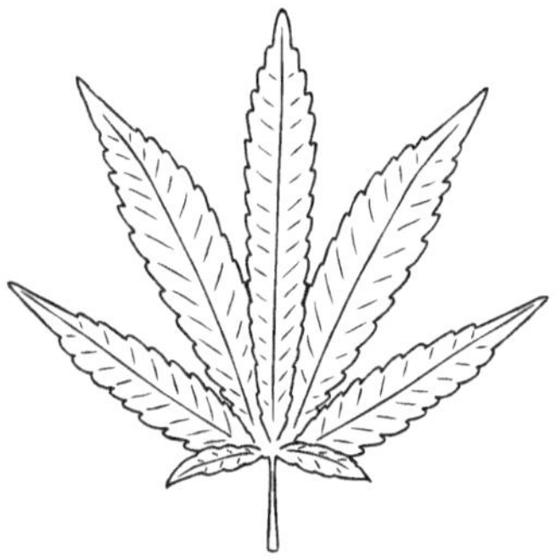

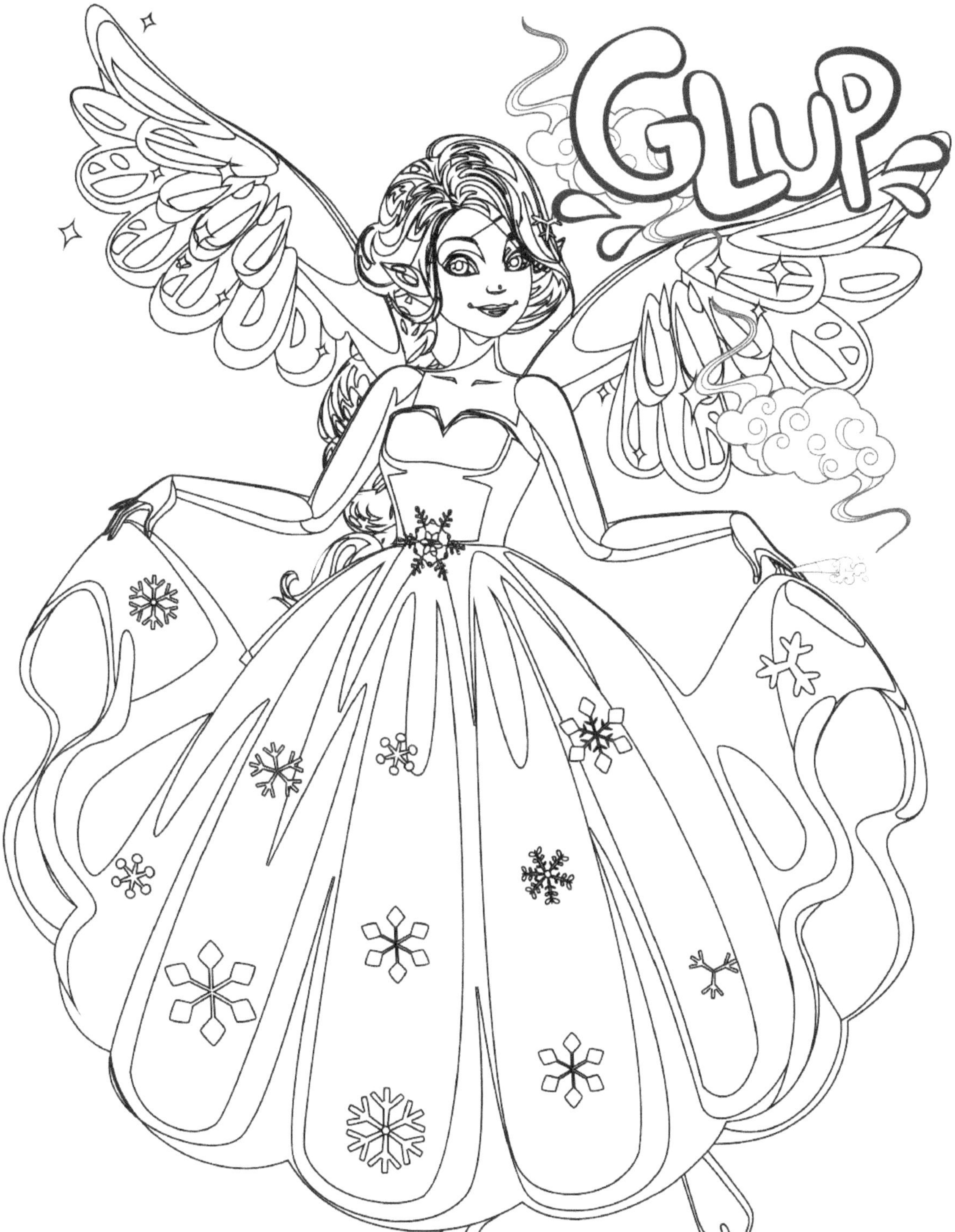
GLUP

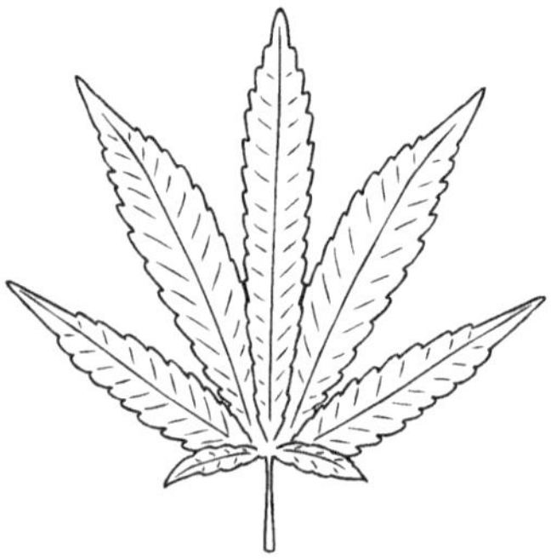

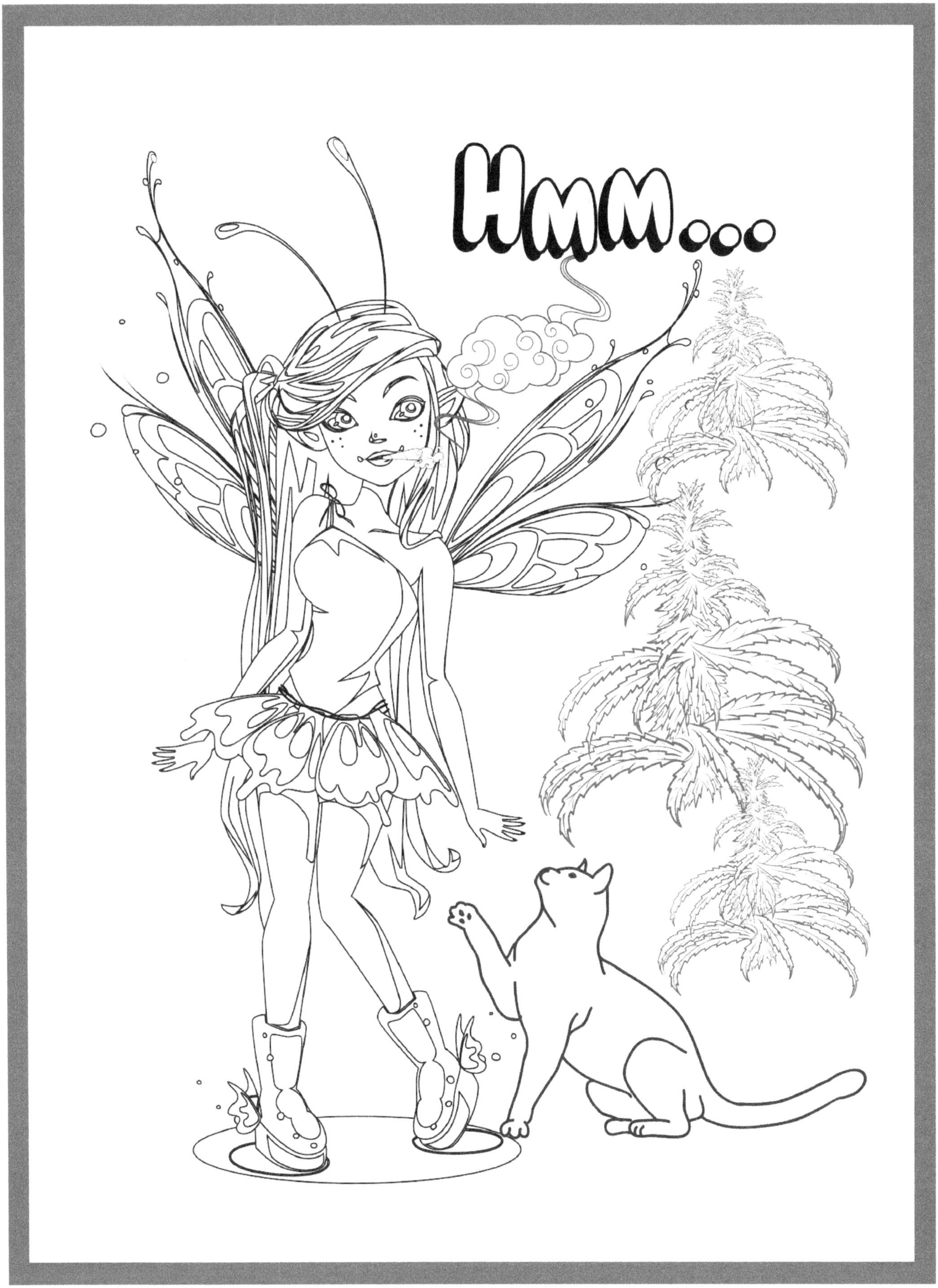
Hmm...

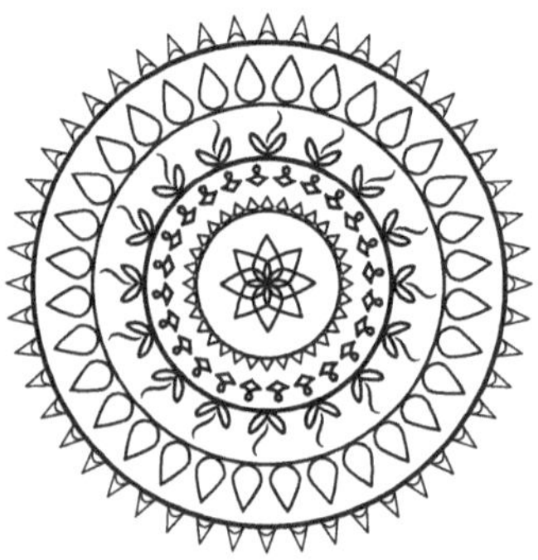

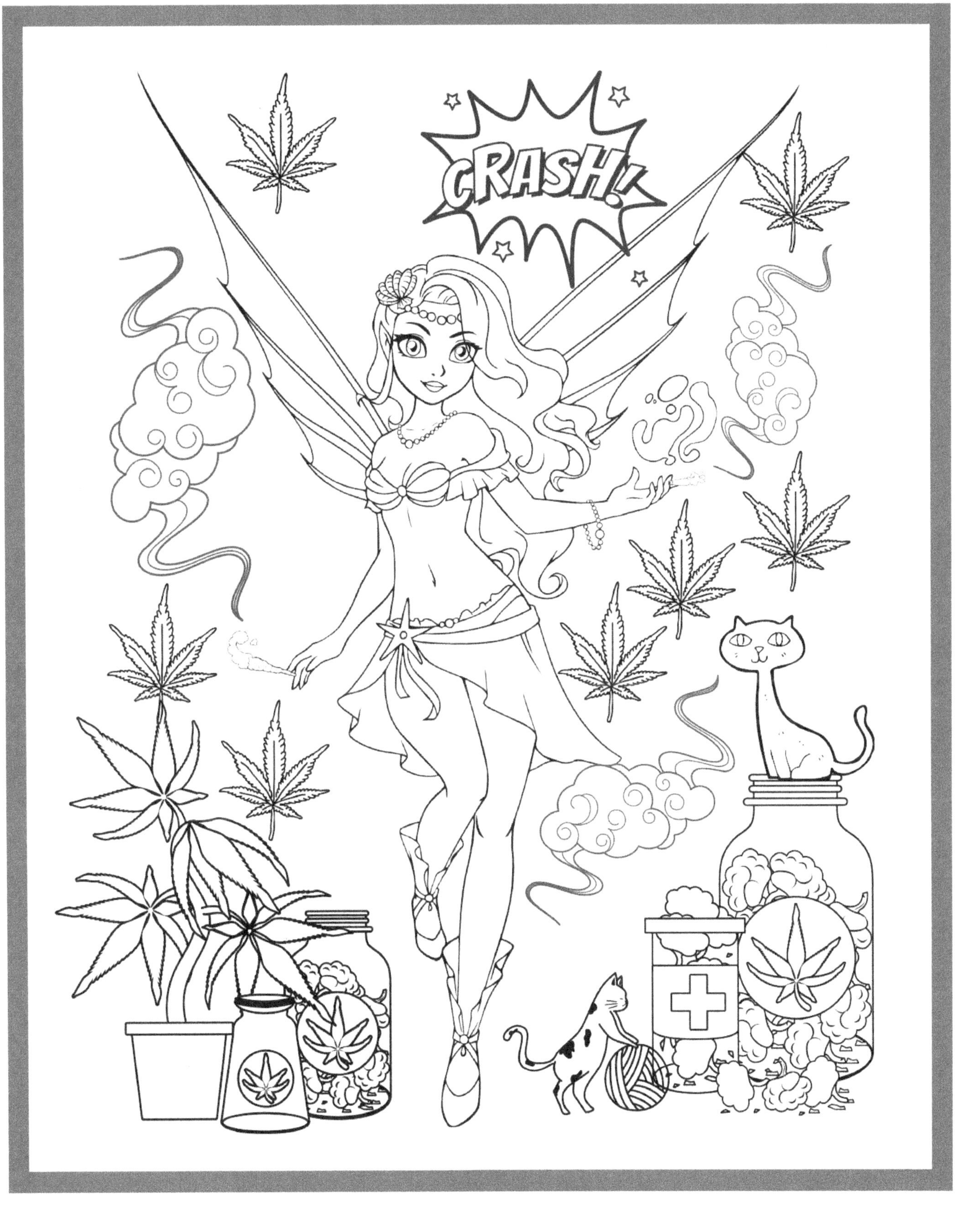
CRASH!

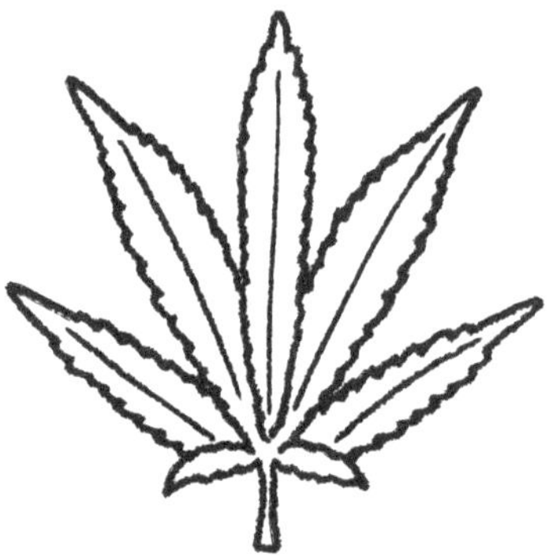

OH YEAH!

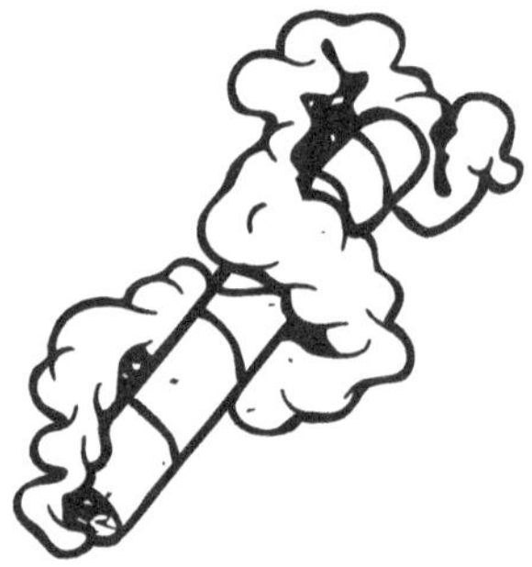

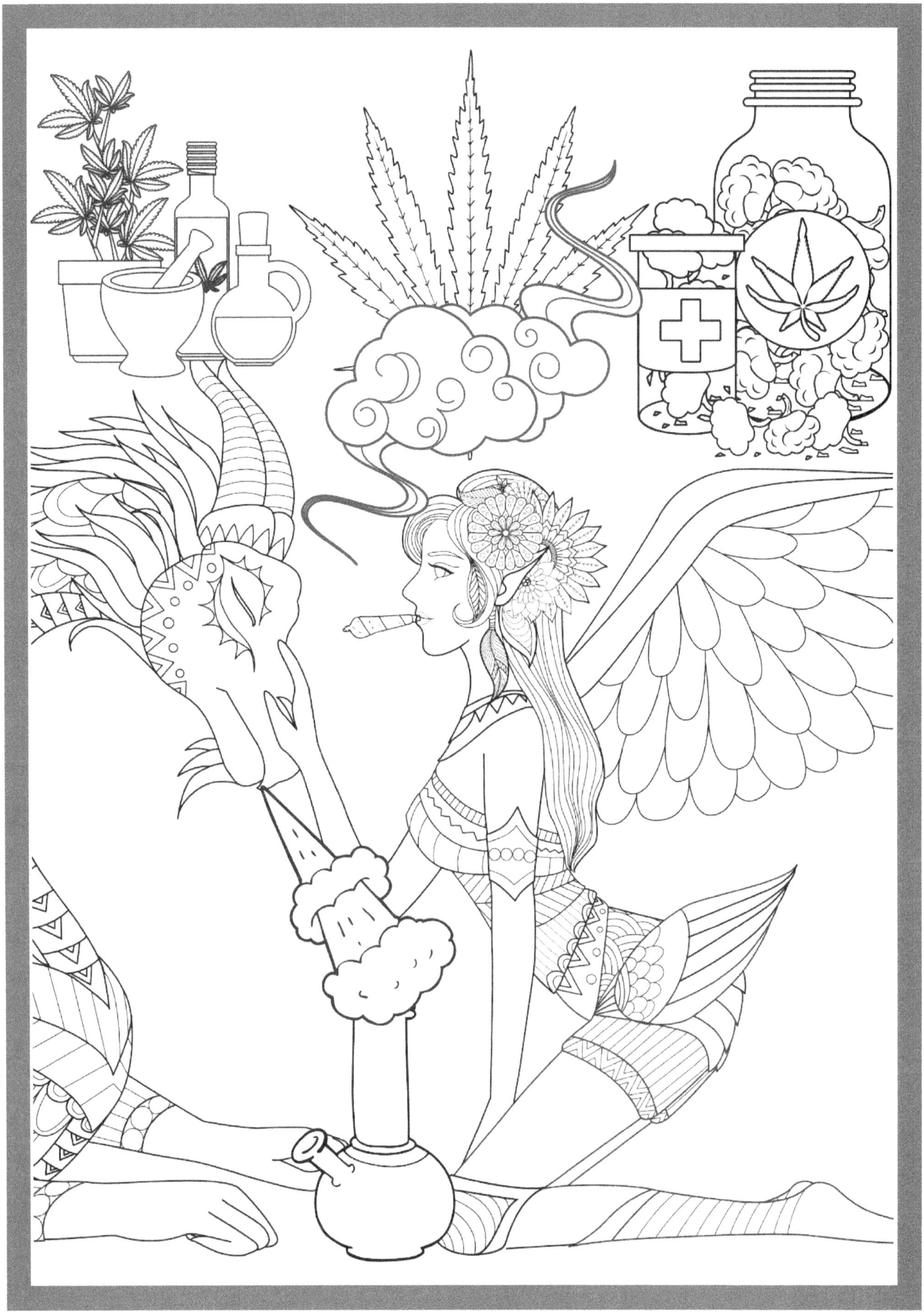

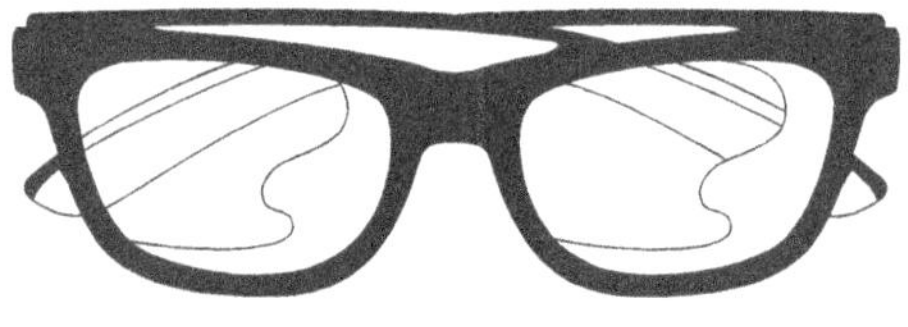

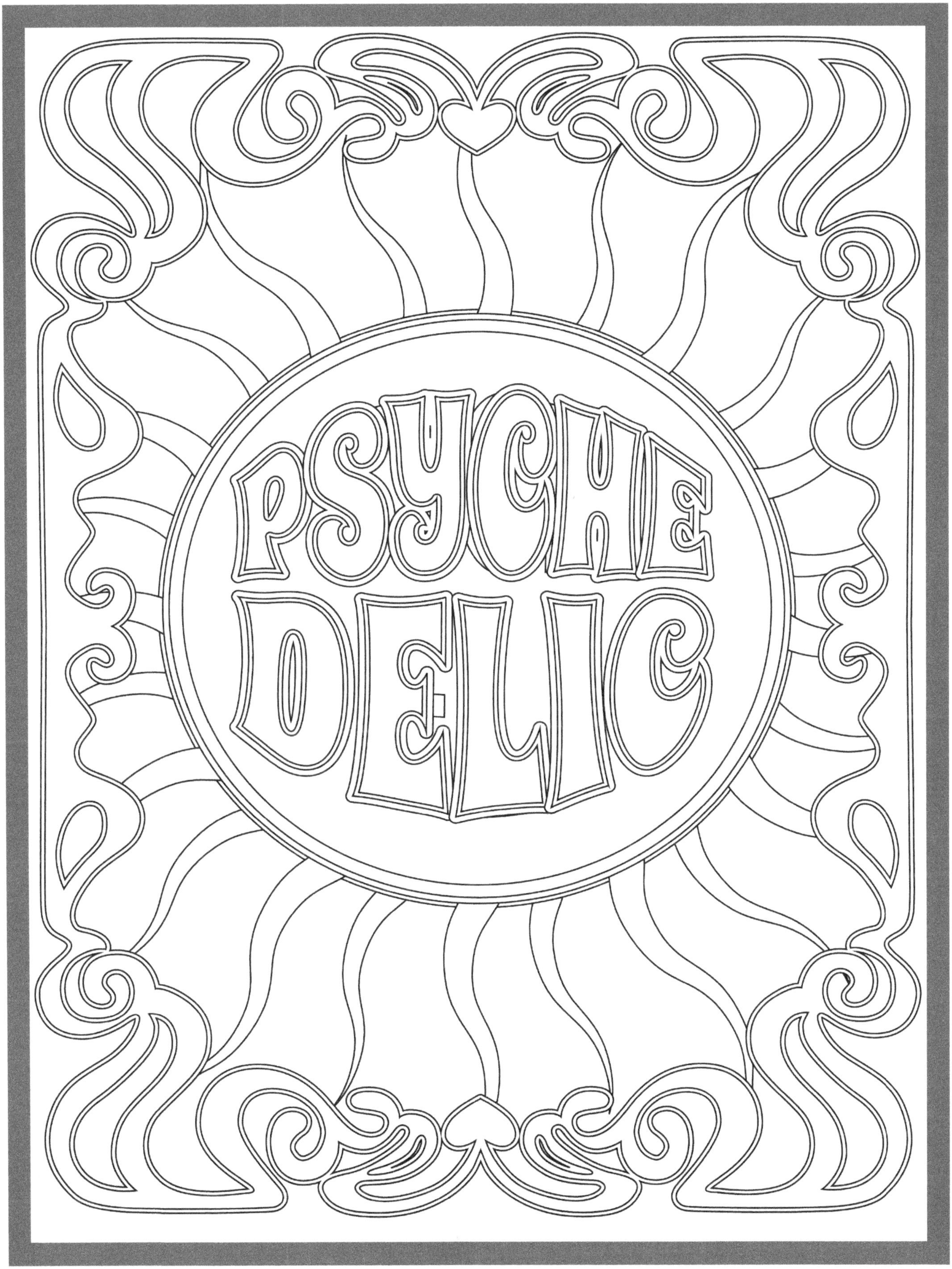
PSYCHE
DELIC

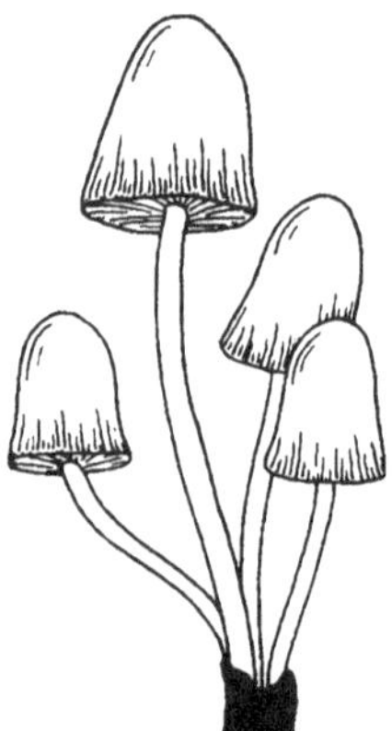

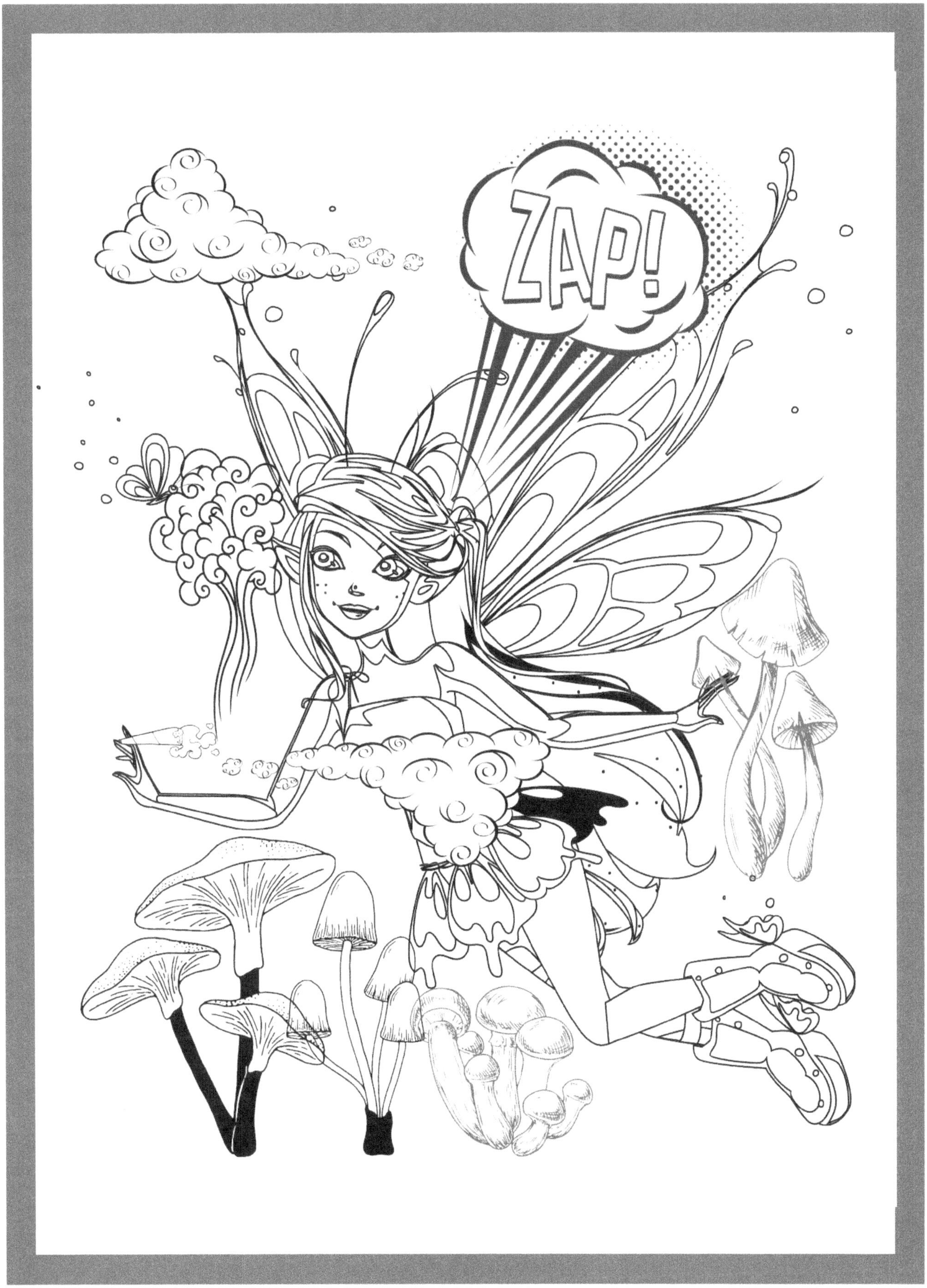
ZAP!

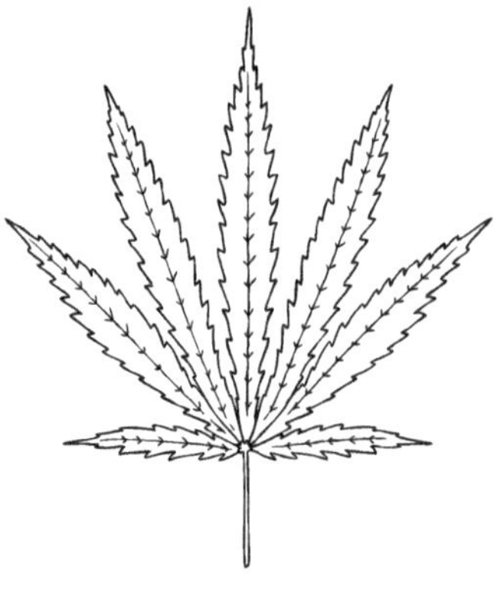

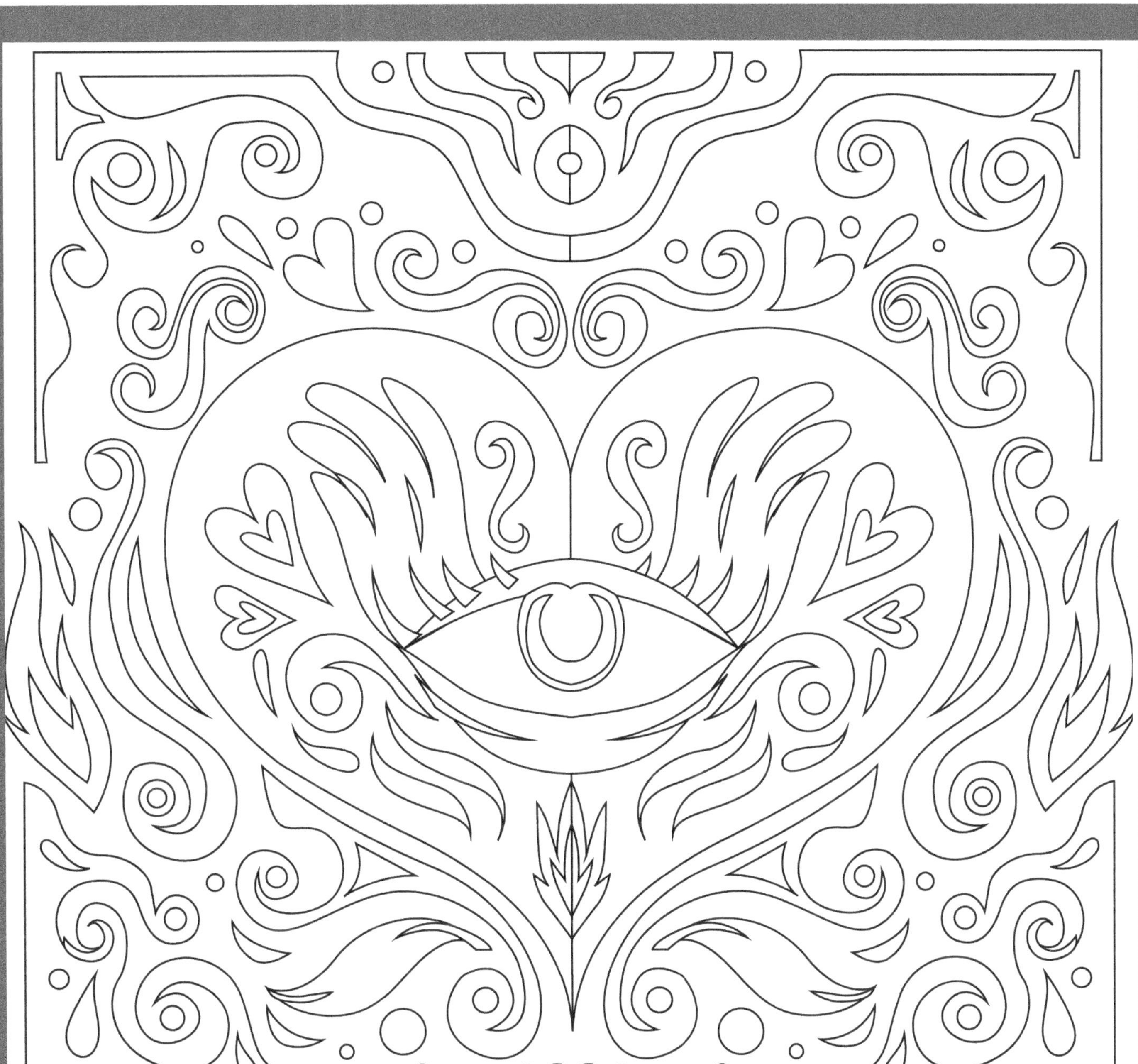
LOVE

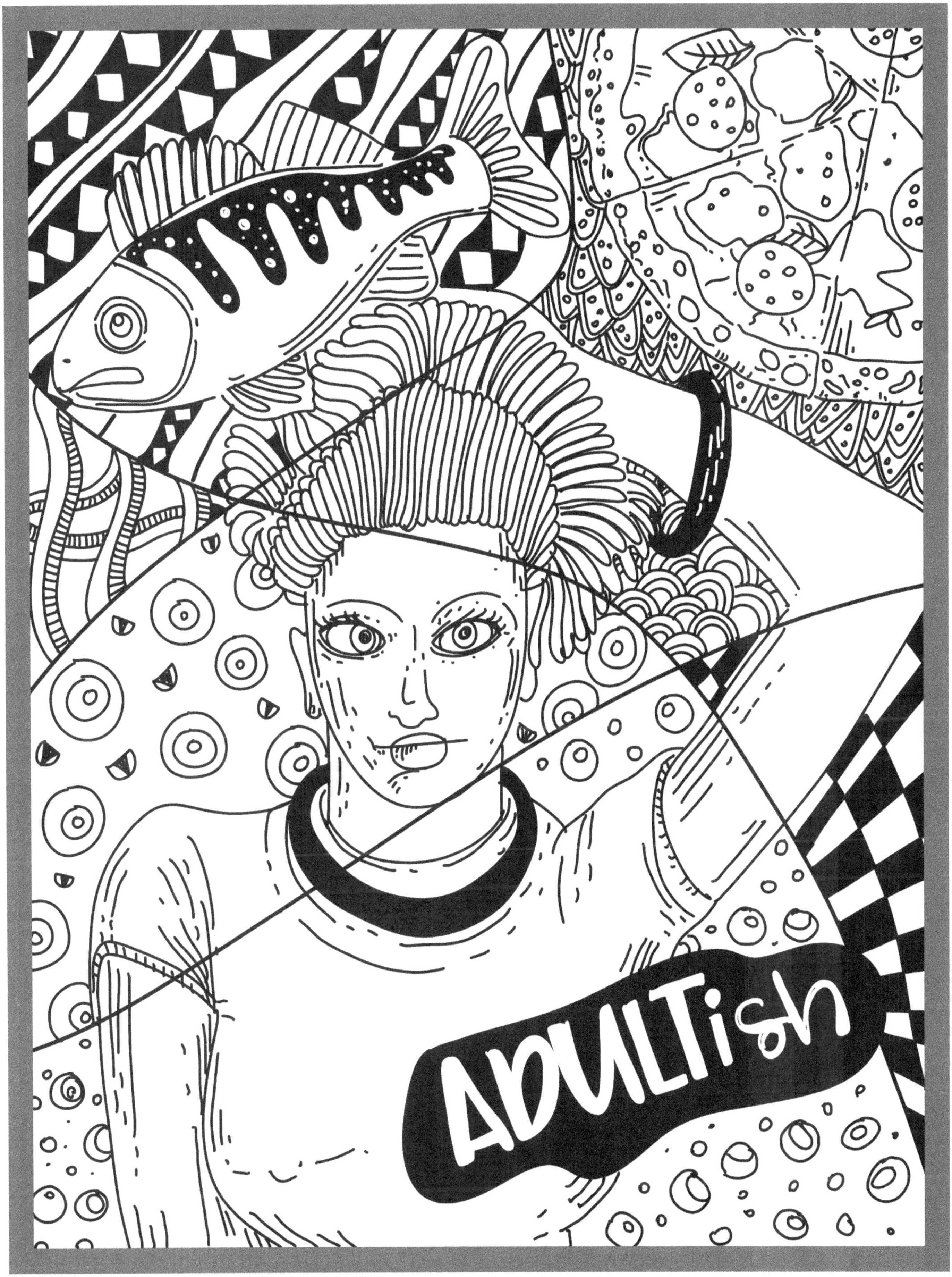
ADULTish

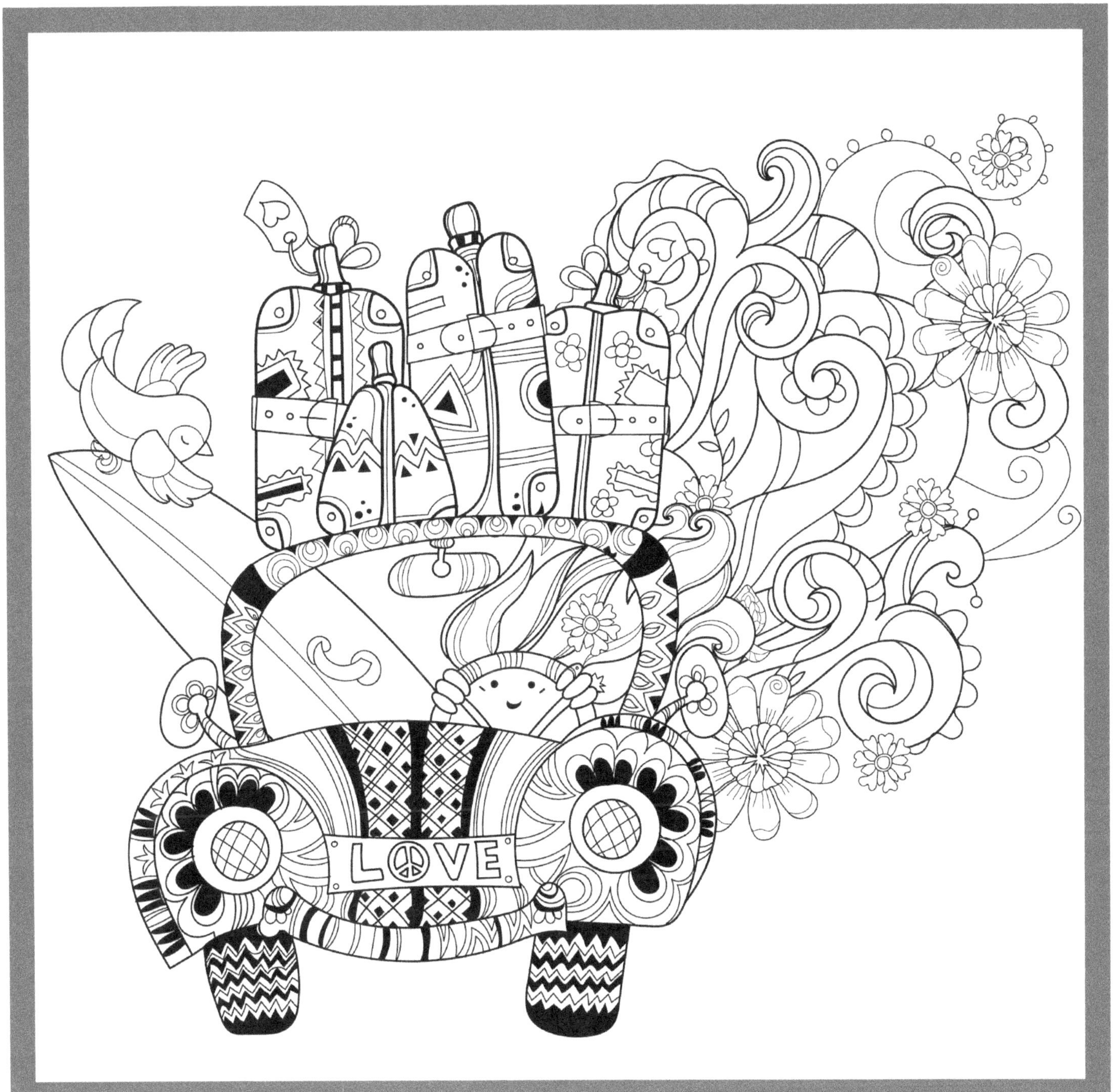
LOVE

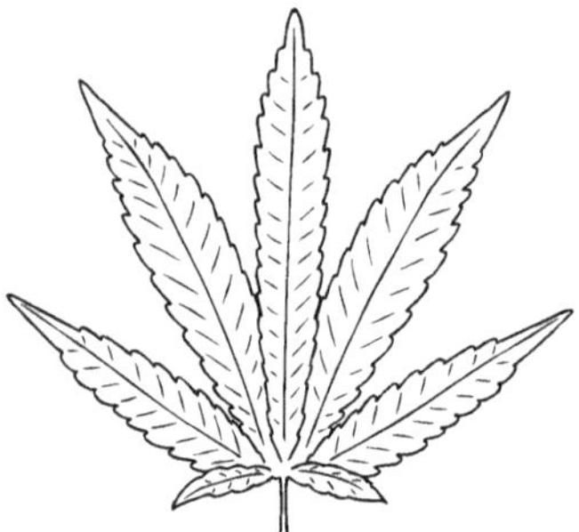

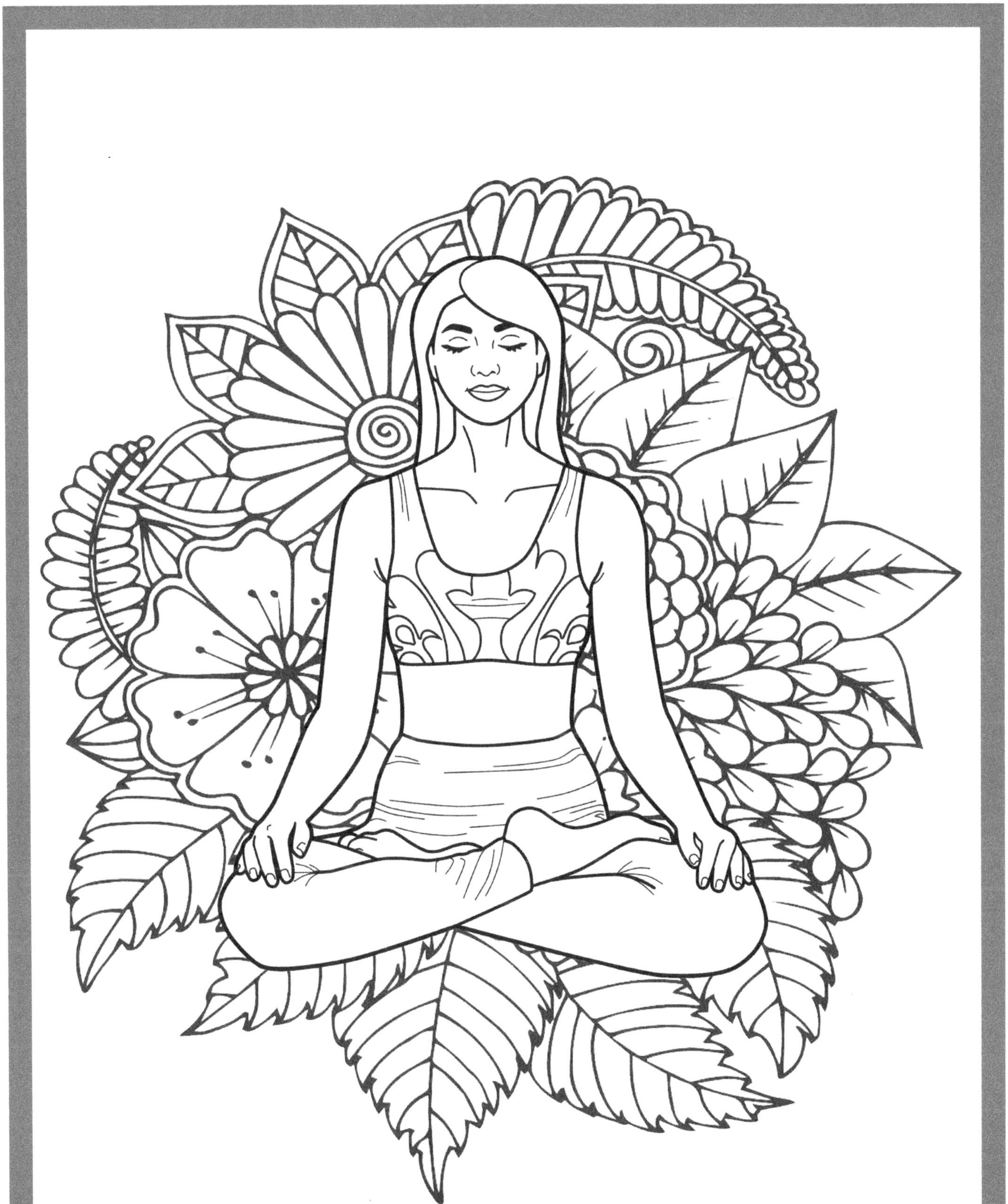

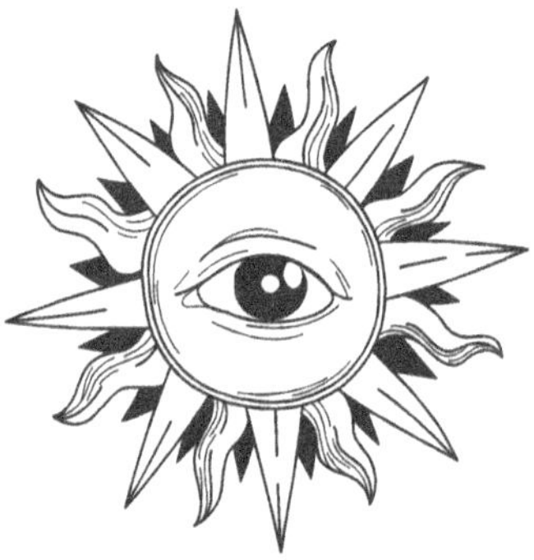

www.ingramcontent.com/pod-product-compliance
Lightning Source LLC
Chambersburg PA
CBHW080959220526
45467CB00008B/2620
* 9 7 9 8 7 0 3 7 7 8 4 1 8 *